SOVIET EDUCATION

SOVIET EDUCATION

ANTON MAKARENKO
AND THE YEARS
OF EXPERIMENT

JAMES BOWEN

THE UNIVERSITY OF WISCONSIN PRESS
MADISON
1962

Published by
The University of Wisconsin Press
430 Sterling Court, Madison 6, Wisconsin

Printed in the United States of America
by Vail-Ballou Press, Inc., Binghamton, N.Y.

Library of Congress Catalog Card Number 62-15591

Much of this study is based on the three major educational writings of Anton Makarenko—*The Road to Life, Learning to Live,* and *A Book for Parents,* to give them their English titles. Each of these books exists in a readily available, authoritative English language translation, issued in each case by the State Foreign Languages Publishing House in Moscow. The practice throughout this study has been to quote from the translation, and the quotations have then been checked against the original to avoid errors in interpretation. The translations of *Learning to Live* by Ralph Parker, and of *A Book for Parents* by Robert Daglish, are extremely competent and appear in quite felicitous prose. *The Road to Life,* translated by the Russians, Ivy and Tatiana Litvinov, is somewhat awkward, although nonetheless accurate; certainly it lacks the elegance of Stephen Garry's translations. However, the Litvinovs' translation is used because they have translated the whole trilogy and not just the first volume, as Garry has done, and their translation, having a wider circulation, is more likely to be available to the reader.

When there has been need to refer to the original Russian, the footnote acknowledges the quote by the Russian title; these are the original titles given by Makarenko and not those invented by the translators. These titles, with their English equivalents, are *Pedagogicheskaya Poema (The Road to Life), Flagi na Bashnyakh (Learning to Live),* and *Kniga dlya Roditelei (A Book for Parents).* The text of all of these books is taken from the 1957 edition of Makarenko's *Sochineniya v Semi Tomakh (Collected Works in Seven Volumes).*

The translations of others are acknowledged in the footnotes; where none is given the translation is my own. In particular I am responsible for the various translations from the *Great Soviet Encyclopedia.*

In transliterating the Russian Cyrillic alphabet into our own Roman letters I have, in general, followed the Library of Congress system (see Note on Transliteration). I am not happy with the transliteration of Makarenko's own name insofar as it leads to mispronunciation. I would like to have transliterated the Russian "e" by "ie." However I cannot go against the practice of the Russians themselves. A reasonably correct pronunciation of his name should have the stress in the middle, and sound something like M'kár-i-enko. The first syllable should not be stressed.

There are a number of individuals and institutions that have assisted this study in various ways and I would like to mention, in particular, the library of the University of Illinois for its excellent professional assistance. I would like to make a special point of referring to the critical reading of the manuscript and the provision of numerous suggestions by Henry Silton Harris of the Department of Philosophy and Archibald W. Anderson of the College of Education, both of the University of Illinois. Finally I wish to thank Isobel Korbel of the University of Wisconsin Press for her very competent and gracious editorial work.

JAMES BOWEN

Calgary, Alberta,
Canada
March 1962

NOTE ON TRANSLITERATION

1. For the following letters I think there is no question whatsoever:

А	A	К	K	Т	T
Б	B	Л	L	Ф	F
В	V	М	M	Х	KH
Г	G	Н	N	Ц	TS
Д	D	О	O	Ч	CH
Ж	ZH	П	P	Ш	SH
З	Z	Р	R	Щ	SHCH
И	I	С	S	Э	E

2. The Russian Е has been transliterated as E, except when it begins a word, when it is transliterated as YE; for example, in the word for "nature," which in Russian appears as ЕСТЕСТВЕННО, it is transliterated as YESTESTVENNO.

3. The Russian Й has been transliterated as I, and the ending ИЙ has been rendered as II. However, when it ends a proper name, I have dropped the second I. For example, ГОРКИЙ appears as "Gorki" and not "Gorkii."

4. The Russian У has been transliterated as U; for example, УРОК is UROK.

5. The Russian Ю has been transliterated as YU; for example, СОЮЗ appears as SOYUZ.

6. The Russian Я I have preferred to transliterate as YA, not as IA. I have kept IYA as the transliteration of the ending ИЯ.

7. The hard sign has been ignored and the soft sign Ь appears as an apostrophe.

CONTENTS

PART I
MAKARENKO AND SOVIET EDUCATION

CHAPTER 1
ANTON SEMYONOVITCH MAKARENKO

In the Soviet Union today the name of Anton Semyonovitch Makarenko is widely known. As a writer of novels, articles, and stories he is known to millions, especially for his serious works devoted to the problems of the upbringing of the child and of home and family relationships. At the same time, his name is current in educational circles, and his lifelong devotion to the causes of Soviet education has earned him the respect of many contemporary Soviet educators. During his all-too brief life (1888–1939), both his practices and his writings in the field of education have secured his name and influence in the development of much present-day Soviet education. What is perhaps a most curious fact, certainly to Western readers, is that his greatest work, an educational treatise, is widely read as literature. This is the remarkable trilogy, *The Road to Life,* which has enjoyed enormous popularity, certainly far beyond that of any comparable book in the West. In the *Great Soviet Encyclopedia* it is recorded that "In 1953 the works of Makarenko were published in eighteen of the languages of the USSR and in many other world languages. *The Road to Life,* becoming one of the favorite books of Soviet readers, has gone through forty-one editions with a total circulation of 1,125,000 copies." [1]

The Road to Life is a remarkable and moving account of
the educational development of a group of young Russian
war orphans after World War I. Indeed, by any standards the
story is a really great study of education. Part of its charm,
especially for nonpedagogically-minded readers, is the simple,
unaffected, intimate prose style in which it is written. Dealing
with Makarenko's own problems with the education of ut-
terly abandoned children, it records very simply and movingly the joys and sorrows, the failures and the successes, the
loves and the hates of the members of the school. And
through the pages the central figure of Makarenko himself
emerges as a tender-hearted, sympathetic man whose life is
devoted to the humble task of making better the lives of
some of those for whom existence would otherwise have
been a travesty of human values. Professor Medinski, of the
Academy of Pedagogical Sciences of the RSFSR, goes so far
in his admiration as to declare that "As a work of literature dealing with education, the book has no equal in the
world." [2]

Overt recognition of Makarenko in the Soviet Union is
overwhelming. His name frequently appears in contemporary
Russian writings in education and psychology, usually in
tones approaching reverence. In a recent set of essays on
education from the Soviet Union, for example, written by
six leading psychologists, recognition of Makarenko's work
appears in five of the six papers.[3] Apart from the constant
stream of reissues of his works that come from the various
state publishing houses, there is an institute concerned with
research into his writings within the Academy of Pedagogical
Sciences, and, in 1951, a museum was established in Kruikov
near the scene of his labors. His life work occupies nearly
three full pages in the most recent issue of the *Great Soviet
Encyclopedia*. And to crown his life's work, he was decorated
with the Order of the Red Banner of Labor for literary
achievement on February 1, 1939, just two months before
his sudden collapse and death. In looking for a name that

has endured in Russian education throughout the period between the two world wars, Makarenko's is one of great stature and lasting significance.

Despite his enormous popularity within the Soviet Union and the considerable influence that his methods are exerting on current Soviet practice,[4] Makarenko is still virtually unknown in the educational literature of the English-speaking world. Indeed, so far as can be ascertained, only two short monographs on him have ever been published in English.[5] The actual problem that Makarenko faced is known to the West, however, through the release in 1933 of the film *Road to Life*.[6] John Dewey appears on the screen to narrate the introduction which is an excellent summary of the film's content. Thus he says that

Ten years ago, every traveler in Russia came back with stories of the hordes of wild children who roamed the countryside and infested the city streets. They were the orphans of soldiers killed in the war, of fathers and mothers who perished in the famine after the war. You will see a picture of their old road to life, a road of vagabondage, violence, thieving. You will also see their new road to their new life, a road constructed by a brave band of Russian teachers.

After methods of repression had failed, they gathered these children together in collective homes, they taught them cooperation, useful work, healthful recreation. Against great odds they succeeded. There are today no wild children in Russia.

You will see a picture of great artistic beauty, of dramatic action and power. You will also see a record of a great historic episode. These boys are not professional actors. They were once wild children, they once lived in an actual collective. You will also see an educational lesson of the power of freedom, sympathy, work and play to redeem the juvenile delinquent; a lesson from which we too may learn.

Unfortunately, despite the use of the title of Makarenko's book, the film does not mention him by name, nor does it in any way recognize the fact that he pioneered the work in this field. There is no doubt, however, that the film is based upon Makarenko's theories and practices. Throughout, the spirit of Makarenko is evident, although many of the episodes have been changed both in form and sequence. Aesthetically the film is most satisfying and is valuable for its ability to convey a sense of immediacy, a feeling of historical presence, and to present the grim realities of the period around 1923 in which it is set. Yet at the same time, it is chiefly concerned in glorifying the paternal benevolence of the Soviet government and in ignoring the individuality and initiative that Makarenko displayed.

The West's continued ignorance of Makarenko would be easy to understand were his writings inaccessible to English-speaking educators. This is not the case, however, and has not been for some time. His three most important works, *The Road to Life, Learning to Live,* and *A Book for Parents,* are all readily available in good English translations, although *Learning to Live* is given to provincial idioms of England that might require some supplementary elucidation for American readers. Indeed, all of the elements of Makarenko's theories can be found in these excellently translated, available works, and for an understanding of his theory there is, at least for the general educator, little need to go beyond them.

There are several recommendations to a study of his work. Apart from his relevance to the obvious upsurge of interest in Soviet education at present, a study of Makarenko, as indeed of any important figure in a period, is a good way to gain an understanding of the history of the period. There is no doubt that the history of Russian education between the two world wars, as recorded in Makarenko's writings, is lively and rich. And he was working at the not inconsiderable task of social reconstruction at the same time that many educators in the English-speaking world, especially in the United States, were also advocating various brands of social reconstruction. It is true, of course, that the banners that gathered in this camp were many and varied, and it is not implied that the social reconstruction attempted by Makarenko is the same as that conceived in our own society. Yet his work will have lessons for us, and by contrast it will point up the more clearly the shape of our own thinking.

In the period in which Makarenko worked, Russia faced enormous educational tasks. On the one hand there was the imperative need to establish and consolidate a new educational system to implement the aims and purposes of the new society, and on the other there was the even more pressing need to make provision for the millions of homeless children who were rapidly becoming one of the most serious social problems of the new era. To neither of these challenges had the Bolsheviks a ready answer. Their revolutionary theories were only the most superficial generalities when it came to the specific problems of education, especially when the educational problem was daily becoming so serious. Makarenko was assigned to the task of directing one of the colonies that had been established to house and care for these homeless war orphans, and it was in this initial period that he set to the task of developing, from the beginnings, a new practice and theory of Soviet education.

MAKARENKO'S LIFE AND WORK

Makarenko's early life was simple and relatively unimportant, although his humble beginnings have been seized upon rather avidly by Soviet propagandists. He was born on March 1, 1888, the son of a painter who worked in the railway workshops in the small Ukrainian railway town of Belopole in the province of Kharkov. One contemporary Russian writer, Kostelianets, has given a deep significance to the father, making of him a semitragic figure. In his critical-biographical study of Makarenko he reports that Makarenko's father, Semen Grigorevitch, had "lost his parents in early childhood, and subsequently followed the cruel school of life, which superimposed a deep impress on all parts of his character. He was a person with a strongly developed sense of proper dignity, as exacting with himself as with others. Strong-willed in his character, Semen Grigorevitch taught himself to read and write with difficulty. Anton Makarenko, many years after the death of his father, depicted him with great respect in *A Book for Parents* and later as the worker Teplov in the novel *Honor*. Anton Makarenko showed his traits to be a love of labor and pride in his work, reserve, exactingness and humanity. Anton Makarenko's mother, Tatyana Mikhailova, was engaged in housekeeping. She was a sociable woman, endowed with a sense of humor." [7]

Despite attempts like this to find in Makarenko the origins of the true proletarian man, there is little need to feel that his life was in any way unusual or different. On the contrary, he seems to have led a normal, full life for a child of his times. Indeed, there is some evidence to suggest that young Anton was by no means content to remain within the working class, insofar as his own educational activities were dominated by the bourgeois urge to "get on."

Due to the highly formalized social system inaugurated by Peter the Great, social mobility was extremely slow, and there were few routes for advancement open to the children of the non-noble classes. One of the most popular methods, as the novels of Tolstoy—among others—reveal, was the army. By diligent application it was possible in the Russia of the time for people of obscure origins to advance at least a certain way socially through military service. Whether this was Makarenko's ambition is not known. What is known, however, was that he always showed a profound admiration for the army and habitually wore a military style of clothing. When he came to organizing his home for war orphans, it soon developed into a sort of quasi-military academy with detachments, ranks, uniforms, and the paraphernalia of army life: sentries, rifles, drums, bugles, and regimental colors.

Certainly he was a most diligent pupil. Kostelianets records that Makarenko was a bright lad whose ability was revealed early, that he had his first education from a neighboring boy who had some degree of literacy—the sole one of the neighboring children who had attended school. And here the qualities of Makarenko's parents were of importance in his scholastic success. To the extent of their means, the parents helped Anton in his desire to study. When the railway workshops were moved in 1900 to the settlement of Kruikov, near Kremenchyg, Anton was sent to the local village school. In an article on *Electoral Rights of the Workers* (1937) Makarenko stated that "My father was a worker and therefore I studied on copper money," referring to the fact that tuition amounted only to small change.[8] Again, in the novel *Honor* Makarenko depicted a scene between the worker Teplov and his son who was about to enter school. The discussion was about grades. " 'Bring home grades of B? . . . You had better not! Only bring home A's. Do you understand?' The father, Semen Maximovitch, expressed himself very clearly. His son, Alexi, was very quick to comprehend, and was equally quick in his mind. Thus it followed that Alexi maintained a straight-A average, at no time giving his father cause to grieve." [9] Kostelianets argues, no doubt rightly, that this was a reflection of the circumstances of Makarenko's own life.[10] At the end of 1904, Anton Makarenko finished the program of the six-year school in Kremenchyg with a straight-A average.

Following that event, he took a one-year course in pedagogy and was appointed on September 1, 1905, as a teacher of the lowest grade to the railway school of Kruikov, the place where he had received his own initial education. He stayed in this post for the next six years, although he was close to losing either his head or his liberty during the revolutionary events of 1905. The young Makarenko was profoundly influenced by the strikes and fiery orations of the Bolshevik agitators who came forward at the meetings held in Kruikov, and so enthused did Makarenko become that he gave an oration himself on the subject of revolution at a teachers' convention in Luibotin Station, then the center of the revolutionary movement on the Kharkov-Nicolaevski railroad. The inevitable result of this revolutionary movement was a cruel persecution by the tsarist government of the more than 20,000 teachers. The majority were discharged, although many were arrested and sentenced to exile. This reaction was intensified during the immediate postrevolutionary years, and even reached Kruikov, where the school superintendent Kompantsev was replaced by a new superintendent who inaugurated a strongly repressive bureaucratic regime.[11]

On September 24, 1911, Makarenko finished at the school of Kruikov and the following day left for a comparable post in a similar railway town school at South Dolinsk in the Khersonski province. He remained there for three years and, as a result of his energetic and capable work, succeeded in gaining admission to the Poltava Teachers' Institute, where he was to continue his teacher education. A further result of this course of training would be to qualify him for higher posts in the teaching service. There is no doubt that his performance there exceeded expectations. The course of training was interrupted for six months when he was inducted into the army on September 20, 1916. However, he was discharged because of weak eyesight the following March 19 and returned to the Poltava Teachers' Institute in time to graduate with the institute's gold medal on June 15, 1917. After two more years back in the railway school of Kruikov he was appointed director of the school in Poltava, a post which he held from September 9, 1919, to September 3, 1920.

Makarenko again commenced to become vocal about the progress and directions of both Soviet society and education. Accordingly, he was summoned, in September of 1920, before the chief of the Provincial Department of Education. As a result of this interview, he accepted the challenge to back up his convictions by assuming the directorship of a residential school for war orphans on the outskirts of Poltava. Makarenko worked in this colony for the next seven years, until he left to organize another colony on similar lines established by the Soviet Police in Kharkov. This task was left in 1935.

In the years immediately following he was able to devote himself to full-time writing. This was a belated attempt to catch up with Makarenko's conscious choice of occupation, that of a writer. He earlier had turned to pedagogical work when Maxim Gorki, to whom he submitted some of his work in 1917, discouraged him in his literary career. While at the Poltava Teachers' Institute, Makarenko had enjoyed some success in having short prose pieces and poems published in the satirical journal *Institutskaya Shchel*. Kostelianets gives a good account of the ensuing action. Flushed with success, Makarenko "sent to Maxim Gorki the story, *A Foolish Day*. In answering the beginning writer, Gorki praised the interesting tale but pointed out artistic weaknesses. 'From that letter I saw very well,' said Makarenko afterwards, 'that to write I knew that it is necessary to learn. However thoroughly and long I learned to write, that re-jection remained deep in my soul. For thirteen years I did not repeat any attempts at publication, and endeavoured not even to think of it.' " [12]

After this thirteen-year period he did indeed begin to publish again, although for a time he confined his efforts to pedagogical and journalistic articles, chiefly destined for small, obscure journals and newspapers. He was, however, to receive considerable encouragement from Gorki to write an account of his educational efforts with the war orphans in the colony of which he was director, and in 1925 he began this work calling it, originally, *Pedagogicheskaya Poema* (*An Epic of Education*), concluding it in 1935. (This book later became known as *The Road to Life*.) From around that period on his readers increased enormously. He was suddenly famous. In the few years before his death, both literary and educational works flowed from his pen. *A Book for Parents* was written in 1937, and during the same period he began the semi-autobiograph-

ical novel *Honor,* finishing it in 1938. Also in 1938 he wrote
Flags on the Battlements, which has been translated into
English under the title of *Learning to Live.* This was published in 1939, and is an account of his work at the second
home for war orphans which he conducted under the auspices
of the Soviet Police. (It is of course more accurate to speak
at the time of this book, the years 1927–35, not of war orphans, but of waifs and delinquents.) In 1940 his *Lectures
on the Education of Children,* also written in 1937, was published. All of his prolific output has been collected, and issued under the general title of *Sochineniya v Semi Tomakh
(Collected Works in Seven Volumes).*

Within the Soviet Union, Makarenko's fame rests securely
on his work in developing a system of education that went
beyond education narrowly conceived as book learning, seeking instead to develop the whole person. Makarenko wanted
to provide for the total all-round growth of his charges and,
if possible, to develop a science of pedagogy that would be
able to employ reliable, predictable methods for producing
and controlling a particular type of personality. That he was
not completely successful in his quest does not by any means
discredit his work. In a lifetime one man can make only a
limited contribution to any discipline, and his contribution
 was neither small nor insignificant. What is important is that
he developed a method and pioneered a way that has become
alive in the minds of current Soviet educators. Many of his
ideas are now being systematically explored and further developed. Obscure and unknown during the twenties, he anticipated many later orthodoxies of Soviet education once
the romantic period of experiment in the twenties ended,
and many of the ideas which he alone inaugurated have become themselves the orthodoxies of Soviet education.

CHAPTER 2

THE BACKGROUND OF SOVIET EDUCATIONAL PROBLEMS

THE IMMEDIATE PROBLEMS OF SOVIET EDUCATION

As the preceding chapter indicated, the Bolsheviks faced some enormous problems on their assumption of power within Russia. Certainly for some years at least their power was held in a precarious balance, and for a period of time it seemed doubtful whether the revolutionary forces could continue to keep control of what was a rapidly disintegrating political and social system. Apart from the military crises which continued, the country faced economic, social, and political challenges to stability. On the social front alone it was imperative to re-establish the normal activities of the people, among which activities were the provisions for education. Apart from the fact that the Bolsheviks inherited an educational system already split by power struggles that were centuries old, a system completely unsuited to consolidate the proposed new regime, there was the problem of displaced human lives. The carnage of the war in Russia was on a colossal scale. Estimates vary, but all agree that the number of people killed ran into many millions. As if this was not tragedy enough, the legacy of this disaster remained—the enormous number of children who had been orphaned, a

13

group amounting to many millions. And the speed with which these people were growing up into "affectless," unintegrated minorities and groups posed a serious threat to the social stability of the new order.

In considering the work of a man like Makarenko and in gaining even a slight appreciation of the magnitude of his accomplishments, it is necessary to see his efforts against the background of the rest of the Bolshevik attempts to get an educational system in operation. This, of course, raises a further issue. That is, the immediate activities of the Bolsheviks in securing an educational system must be seen against the wider background of the development of Russian education in general. Pares has continually stressed in his writings on Russia the necessity of understanding the historical development of the people. Any attempt to understand the Russians, especially with respect to the immediate postrevolutionary years, is bound to be inadequate unless it takes into account the long-term development of their culture and history.[1] Certainly much of the evaluation of Russian reforms and actions has been considerably ill-judged because of this failure to account for the necessary historicity of many movements. Also, it is difficult to find many accounts of Russian education written in the twenties or thirties that are not tinged with some form of special pleading.

In considering and appreciating Makarenko it is important to remember that his own life completely straddled the two regimes. Born under the tsarist order, he was educated within the dual system of the time. Having been brought up in the stratified social system of the monarchical regime, at the age of seventeen he was already ideologically embroiled in the abortive revolutions of 1905. His teacher training was completed under the old methods, and when the revolution began he had just turned twenty-nine. Then for the remaining twenty-one years of his life he was to be concerned with the task of attempting to reconstruct a new educational system in place of the one that he had repudiated. It would be difficult to understand what he was doing without knowing the assumptions on which he based, both overtly and implicitly, his own actions.

Although the Bolsheviks were able to make many sweeping changes, these could only occur first at the Decree level. Changing human habits is a much slower and more tedious business. The results were that for at least a decade the old system dogged the Bolshevik efforts, and in the thirties, when the whole political order had been firmly founded, a considerable shift back to old habits occurred. If nothing else, the history of Russian education, with the struggle for power by the various authorities, will cast much light on the confusion and anarchy that beset the early efforts at educational reform.

THE STRUGGLE FOR POWER IN
THE HISTORY OF RUSSIAN EDUCATION

When the Bolsheviks came to power in 1917 they made little real break with established Russian tradition. It is true, of course, as this chapter and the following one will show, that they made many sweeping changes of administrative patterns, and they established many things in principle. Nevertheless, their first actions in office were little more than actions which culminated a process that had been occurring for several centuries. For at least the preceding four centuries there was in existence a movement toward a centralized, bureaucratized educational administration.

From the beginnings of organized education in Russia there is a history of repeated attempts by the central government to bring the various educational authorities under its aegis. Whether this central government was tsarist or Bolshevik is beside the point, for in practice both have been despotic in aim. The story of this struggle is long and involved and does not present an orderly, systematic sequence. For a long time the central government was hampered by inefficient lines of communication, by an ineffective civil service, and by the quiet, passive, but real resistance of the vast mass of the peasantry. Indeed, up to the late nineteenth century more than ninety per cent of the population were peasants, and one estimate puts the percentage of all peasants as high as 94.5 at the beginning of the nineteenth century.[2] With a population composition of this order it was always difficult to get reforms beyond the level of the ukaz or edict. Most frequently, reforms failed to become established.

Despite problems of this nature, however, the control of education in Russia has slowly and surely come under a single centralized authority. The advent of the Bolsheviks in 1917 only hastened, in a signally dramatic fashion, a process that was already in operation. The educational movements of the period between the two world wars were, then, a direct development of much that had gone before. Of course, the Bolsheviks sought to make their own innovations, but all too frequently they were not sure of the manner in which their innovations could be implemented. The relation between a socialist ideology on the one hand, and the pedagogical procedures necessary for its realization on the other, was still completely unknown. In a feverish burst of activity to find that relation, Russian educators tried everything, including the most violently individualistic programs that Western nations had to offer.

In the 1929 publication of *The New Education in the Soviet Republic,* the President of the Second State University of Moscow, Albert Pinkevitch, stated in the preface that

the mere enumeration of the names of Hall, Dewey, Russell, Monroe, Judd, Thorndike, Kilpatrick and many others, known to every educator in our country, is a sufficient reminder of the tremendous influence which American education has exerted upon us. In spite of the undoubted differences in ideology which divide soviet from western educational leaders, mutual understanding and recognition of scientific attainments are indispensable. Even in order to condemn one must understand. We have found in the works of American pedagogues and pedologists a rich source of materials. Let us but recall the Dalton Plan, the project method, standard tests, and measurements. All of these innovations have been introduced into our country, even though in their fundamental assumptions they may not be acceptable to us. We, however, do not resort to wholesale condemnation. On the contrary, we study carefully and transplant upon our soil whatever of value we may find elsewhere. And today, I wish to repeat, the most valuable source of such materials is found in the writings of American scientists.[3]

This was written in the period called by George Counts the romantic period of Russian education. This was the period of "internationalization." Later, when Communism began to retreat behind a stronger, less penetrable nationalistic front, many of the experimental innovations mentioned by Pinkevitch were forcefully dropped and rudely denounced. Many reputations were ruined in the thirties when the tide of educational thought was running strongly counter to the earlier ideas of experiment.

From the beginning Makarenko was suspicious of this wholehearted exploration of Western methods. As early as 1925 he voiced his uneasiness at the psychological approach to education, and he was quick to denounce the thinking which held that American methods were a solution to Russian problems. From the beginning he advocated the development of a system of education geared especially to the attainment of socialist objectives. While Makarenko was a vigorous experimenter himself, he sought continually to better serve the ends of Communism, and not to experiment with methods which would lead to unknown outcomes. Thus, unlike Dewey, he believed education was not its own end but remained completely instrumental in the achievement of the truly socialist state. The great contrast between educators like Dewey and Makarenko—both concerned with social reconstruction—lies in the assumptions on which each based his practices. With Makarenko there was never any criticism of the philosophical bases of knowledge or of the

learning proce s. He always implicitly accepted the separation of the knower and the known, and thus he was able to
direct his expe imental work in the service of selecting suitable materials and pedagogical methods to assist in the
achievement o socialist society. And this of course means
that he depended on the Russian tradition in education far
more than he realized. Far from being the innovator that he
thought he was Makarenko was the happy inheritor of a vast
educational process that had been in operation for quite some
time.

THE BEGINNING OF RUSSIAN EDUCATION

Before the sixteenth century formal provisions for education were completely unorganized. Illiteracy was almost universal and ever those classes, such as the clergy, that ought
to have been literate were not. This illiteracy of the clergy
led to the first significant landmark in educational development. In the year 1551 the one hundred main members of
the church met to consider the problem and its possible solution. Despite the enthusiastic decision produced by this meeting—to extend the provisions for education—progress was
scarcely discern ble and the changes made were in the direction of making the teaching of the scriptures and church
dogma more efficient. And education, for what it was worth,
remained in the hands of the clergy.

In this period the first of the educational authorities in
Russia came in o power—the church. Rome, anxious to return Russia to its fold, had begun a campaign spearheaded
by the Jesuits, and in Central Europe, particularly in Poland,
they enjoyed considerable success. Not wishing to let the matter go by default, the Orthodox Church turned its attention
to educational methods designed to counter the Jesuits. The
Metropolitan of Kiev, Peter Mogila, accordingly founded a
Jesuit-style college in Kiev, the purposes of which were "to

teach free knowledge in Greek, Slavonic, Latin, at the same time preserving the truths of Eastern Orthodoxy." [4]

Then, in the reign of Peter the Great, the second of the authorities arose, the state. In response to the crying need to supply educated people to implement his program of Westernization, Peter established the Moscow School of Mathematics and Navigation in 1701 and subsequently, in 1715, the Naval Academy at St. Petersburg. Along with this, Peter formed the civil service. In this respect he began the foundations of the great Russian bureaucratic system which was to be the legacy of the Bolsheviks and which was to sustain them in the early precarious days. Teachers were declared to be civil servants and were accorded places in the neatly detailed civil service hierarchy.

A State Elementary Education Department was created and in each province two schools were established. They were free as well as compulsory, and were designed to teach the basic skills. However this ukaz of 1719 was largely ineffective, due in large part to a grave shortage of teachers. Accordingly, Peter moved to secure his intentions by another route. He proposed to organize the church schools as part of the state system. And so began the struggle for control in Russian education, with the state seeking to assume command of the entire enterprise. In 1721 Peter was successful in abolishing the Patriarchate; the Holy Synod, with a layman public servant as its head, was substituted as the governing body of the church. In this way the church became a department of the civil service and church teachers became civil servants. At the same time each bishop was required to establish elementary schools in his eparchy and to put them under the direct control of Holy Synod. Despite his success here, however, the church schools retained their dominantly ecclesiastical character and they were still far from absorbed into a single monolithic system.

In the following years, this system evolved itself still further and rather haphazardly. In 1775 Catherine II founded the Eoards of Public Assistance whose duty it was to establish and maintain schools in all towns and in the large villages. These boards were supplemented in 1782 by the Commission for the Establishment of Schools whose task it was to equip the schools, primarily with teachers and books. Thus Catherine, perhaps unwittingly, formed the third authority, the local boards, completing the triangle which was to struggle during the next century or so for educational power.

Even under Catherine II there was still no efficient, single centralized authority. Education remained in the hands of the various authorities, each responsible in some manner, often vague, to the tsar. As yet the three bodies—Holy Synod, the local school commissions and the boards of public assistance—all held semi-autonomous authority, and there were no direct lines of communication and responsibility.

Her successor, Alexander I, through the creation of the Ministry of Public Enlightenment, attempted to create a permanent national system of schools. Unfortunately, his reforms were not carried through; each of the various educational authorities clung tenaciously to its power. When he was succeeded in 1825 by the reactionary Nicholas I, much of the spirit of reform disappeared, education languished for want of care, and the rivalries continued unchecked. It was not until Alexander II succeeded Nicholas in 1855 that further progress occurred. Alexander II, however, could do little more than contain the position until 1864, when he moved to organize and consolidate the existing situation on a more rational basis. Thus he created local elective councils, the zemstvos, who assumed some responsibility for education. Being dominated by the large landowners, the zemstvos were not very sympathetic to education for the peasants; and yet, during the following thirty years, they found themselves in the position of supporting the peasants and resisting the tsar.[5] Already in control of three of the four educational agencies, the tsar attempted to put the zemstvos under his direct control. When the zemstvos resisted this successfully, they gained some distinct ascendence in authority.

Nicholas II, who succeeded Alexander in 1894, moved to crush the growing independence of the zemstvos. For their part, they began campaigning actively against the government and in their successive congresses passed resolves of solidarity against any encroachment on or restriction of their power. In 1902 they merely condemned the government; in 1903 they passed a resolution calling for the prior submission of all governmental decisions on education to the zemstvos for their approval; and in 1904 they formed the Union of Liberation (Soyuz Osvobozhdenia) which sought the constitutionalization of all Russia. The resolution was indicative of the advancing spirit of the times, and this sort of mood was beginning to arise in all kinds of organized pressure groups.

After the disgraceful attempts to suppress the popular movement that culminated in "Bloody Sunday" in 1905, a wave of strikes and popular unrest caused the government to promise certain constitutional reforms and to call a representative congress of the people, a duma. The zemstvo schools were in a powerful position. They had been able most successfully to challenge the church schools, chiefly, according to one authority, because they were superior in the two matters of teacher training and teacher salaries.[6] To meet this growing challenge, the government enacted a ukaz which so raised the minimum provisions for education that it seemed likely that the zemstvos would lose control of their schools by default. The zemstvos were equal to the task, however, and managed to retain control until 1914. Then, in that year the Minister for Education, the much-disliked Kasso, published the Ordinance of February 2nd which controlled the zemstvo schools more tightly without completely destroying them. By the provisions of the ordinance, the ministry assumed the right to appoint and dismiss zemstvo teachers; it required

all correspondence to pass through the school district inspector; it empowered itself to reverse zemstvo decisions,
forbade the zemstvos to interfere in the educational and in-
structional provinces of the school, and declared all school
property to belong to the government.[7]

This time strong efforts were made to enforce the ordinance, and the government was now in any case strong
enough to force the issue. The bureaucratization of Russia
had proceeded simultaneously in other areas, and the country had become more amenable to this sort of centralized
control. However, this centralized administration still lacked
any completely unified character, as the confusion and over-
lapping of authority immediately following the Bolshevik
coup was to demonstrate.

By 1914, with respect to past achievements, the educational balance sheet was particularly impressive. Standards
had been raised considerably, the schools offered a wide variety of curricula to an ever-increasing number of children
from all social classes, and the ministry, after centuries of
struggle, had become all powerful. Four types of primary
schools existed, and the secondary schools, for their part,
were also well advanced. They had been opened to all, regardless of social class, and according to Ignatiev it seems
that the peasant children really did, in some measure, attend
them. Although private control of secondary schools had
been made so difficult that the attendance of all but the most
ardent was discouraged, the public school system grew and
became diversified.

EDUCATION IMMEDIATELY PRIOR TO
THE REVOLUTION

It was World War I that hastened the end for the tsarist
regime. Russia had entered that war prepared to fight a
nineteenth-century battle with a large body of parade-ground

trained troops led by aristocratic officers, derided by their men as "squires in uniform." When this feudal sort of army was ranged against the literate, technically trained German host, the slaughter of the Russians was frightful. They suffered nearly four million casualties in the first year alone, and by 1915 the regular army was in large part gone, to be replaced by a relatively inexperienced and useless militia.

Much of the fault lay in the attitude of the government toward the army, which in turn came from the prevailing views of social life. The division of society into rigid classes, each with its own style of life, proved to be the undoing of the social system and, in turn, of the educational system. The Russian strategists realized too late that the army must be developed along new lines. Indeed, literacy was so rare that most Russian troops were unable to write home, even if their families could read. As if this was not a sufficiently demoralizing fact in itself, these vast numbers of ignorant, illiterate peasants were being transported around to places of which they had never previously heard. For many, the travel experiences of the war produced the first inklings of a world that existed beyond their own villages.

Kasso was forced to resign at the end of 1914 and was replaced by Count Paul Ignatiev, a liberal and progressive minister. Knowing that he had the support of the people, Ignatiev made bold efforts to reform education. Profoundly influenced by John Dewey, he based many of his reforms on Dewey's notions of the school and society. Despite the air of urgency, Ignatiev sought to build up an educational system which was carefully and consistently organized around the cooperation of both public and private interests, and based on the wishes of parents. The teacher was central to his ideas of reform and he sought to ensure in the new system that "the teacher must be placed in such a position as to be able to derive a moral satisfaction from his work." [8]

No doubt due to the emergency created by the war rather

than to deliberate policy, Ignatiev was anxious to move toward an even further decentralization of the school system and in the direction of increasing local authority. Thus, in an ordinance of September 25, 1915, he expressed full confidence in the school boards and gave them wide scope in the improvement of school life. He instructed the boards to reorganize moral education and to use moral suasion rather than external discipline. The curriculum was lightened and he improved methods of supervising and estimating pupil progress, instructing the schools to consider the whole individual and his peculiarities.

Much of the reform initiated by Ignatiev, however, remained at the ordinance level and in his two years of office he was unable to achieve any amelioration of the tragedy that was befalling Russia. By this time the army was sadly defeated and the generals were commanding what amounted to semi-autonomous groups with little integration in an overall strategy. At home there was mounting opposition from high officials toward Ignatiev's reforms, especially his liberal tendencies, and intrigue against him was increased. Scarcely two years after he assumed office, Ignatiev resigned on December 27, 1916.

After this education languished even more sadly. Routine was neglected, school morale declined. Disciplinary problems in the school increased and in some secondary schools, Tiflis and Simferopol, for example, strikes occurred. In this sorry state the schools drifted through the tragic year of 1917 while various groups struggled for the control of Russia. Following the abdication of Nicholas and the subsequent failure of the Grand Duke Michael to rally support, power went from the Provisional Government to the infinitely more organized Lenin and his Bolsheviks. The peasants moved in on the nobles' lands, and this "vast process went on of itself through one of the most beautiful autumns ever remembered in Russia. The land was just taken; the livestock too. The peasants came with their carts, and if they did not set fire to the manor, they rifled its contents in a rough and ready division, in which the strongest fared the best. By the end of the year the change was practically complete, and all that was needed was a government that would legalize it." [9]

During its brief reign of power, the Provisional Government made a few changes in the administration of the educational system, attempting to transfer more power to local authorities. In a decree of May 8, 1917, the Provincial and District Councils of Primary Education, whose offices had been filled by the nominees of the government, were abolished and their powers transferred to the local authorities. In a further decree of September 26, 1917, the local authorities were given the right to appoint their own inspectors. In this way the ideals of Ignatiev were implemented in part, although from different motives.

On the eve of the assumption of power by the Bolsheviks the educational scene was particularly confused. The steady growth of power by the central authority had been halted temporarily by Ignatiev, who saw increased emphasis upon individual initiative and autonomy as the only solution to Russia's problems. Then, in a spirit of animosity toward the upper classes, the Provisional Government sought to decentralize education even further. At a time when greater control was needed, effort became widely dispersed. But then the same malaise was afflicting all of Russian corporate life and on October 25 it was a relatively simple matter for the Bolsheviks to assume control of the government.

Bolshevism came in on an excessive wave of idealism, and it needed for its continued success a period of consolidation. Foremost among the instrumentalities available for this purpose was that of education. Yet the educational system that they inherited was completely unsuited to their purposes. Unorganized, controlled by various bodies, separated into a dual system of upper-class and lower-class curricula, it had little to offer the Bolsheviks in the way of a sure instrument to achieve their purposes. The result was that the Bolsheviks set out boldly to forge an instrument, one of truly socialist education. The beginnings were not to be found in the past, that much was clear. Some thought that they lay in the present, and a large group of Soviet educators looked to current methods outside Russia. Others, like Makarenko, kept their gaze firmly inside their own country's borders and tried to make education a specifically nationalistic weapon.

In the next few years, then, the Bolsheviks addressed themselves to the task of determining policy and forging a new school system. The task proved no easy one and instead of taking a few months, as they had thought it would, it followed an agonizing, conflicting course for the next twenty years. As the period wore on, many of the early names disappeared, while that of a relatively obscure teacher from Poltava became more and more prominent. By the time the struggle ended, Makarenko had become one of the leading figures in the development of Soviet education during the period.

CHAPTER 3
THE DILEMMA OF SOVIET EDUCATION

IMMEDIATE CHANGES BY THE BOLSHEVIKS

It seems clear, from the evidence available, that the Bolsheviks had fairly definite ideas on the reform of the educational structure even before they were in control of the government. The administrative pattern, at least, along with certain fundamental principles of policy, had been hammered out in earlier meetings when they still formed an opposition. Certainly within a matter of weeks of their assumption of power there appeared a set of official documents on educational policy. As early as December 24, 1917, they issued their first decree on education which stated that

On the 25th of October, 1917, the entire state power was taken over by the Government of Workers and Peasants. The latter has given over all the Ministries to the Peoples' Commissaires. The Ministries are re-named Peoples' Commissariats.[1]

In this document the fundamental principles of educational policy, in briefest outline, are given. In sum, they amounted to an insistence on universal compulsory education; a much greater provision for education at all levels—kindergarten, college, university, and home education coming in for especial mention; provision for scientific and experimental work; and the intensification of school building and teacher-training programs.

27

To implement this, a new hierarchy was established. In line with the ideological premise of control of the whole nation proceeding from the local soviets, they set about creating new local authorities. As the U.S. Commissioner for Education stated in his 1918 *Report*, "The dictatorship from above, so characteristic of prerevolutionary Russia, gave way to a new order of things, 'the democratization of education.' " [2] All educational authorities were stripped of their powers and the control of the schools was handed over to local Departments of Peoples' Education. In a further decree [3] Article 10 reads:

The direction of affairs connected with peoples' education, such as primary education and self-instruction outside the academic walls, with the exception of higher education, is entrusted to Departments of Peoples' Education, appropriately organized in Executive Committees: Regional, Provincial, County and Volost.

These formed a hierarchical pyramid, resting upon the smallest units, the volosts.

At the top was the State Commission of Education which served as the highest integrating body. In reality it was an all-powerful centralized authority which exercised complete control over the direction of education. The State Commission was composed of the People's Commissar as chairman, his assistant, the five members of the Commissar's Collegium, the chief clerk of the Commissariat, three representatives of the teachers' union, two representatives of the trade unions, one representative of the Bureau of Labor, and one representative of the Central Culture Organization. Their duties, by this decree were, among other things,

The formation of a general plan of Peoples' Education in the Russian Socialist Federal Republic, and the establishment of fundamental principles governing peoples' education, as well as those of school reconstruction; the co-ordination of cultural activities in the localities; the drafting of a budget and the distribution of funds appropriated for common federal cultural needs; as well as other matters of fundamental significance submitted for consideration to the State Commission by the Commissariat's Collegium.[4]

Section 8 of the same document empowered the State Commission to

call and convene, periodically, an All-Russian Congress of Education, to which it submits a report of its activity, and to whose consideration it submits for discussion questions of great importance coming within the jurisdiction of the State Commission.

By the middle of 1918, less than twelve months after taking over the control of power, the new shape of the administration began to emerge. And it came, incidentally, at a time when the greatest possible strains were being put on the central government from without. All through 1918 opposition to Bolshevik rule grew, and at times they were defending their position on as many as fourteen different military fronts. (The attacks, fortunately for the Bolsheviks, were sporadic, independent, and uncoordinated, and with the general armistice of 1918 much of the pressure on them was eased.) Nevertheless, great consolidation of the educational position was achieved. In June of 1918 the first People's Commissar of Education, Lunacharski, was able to issue his first annual report. In the opening words he asserted clearly that the rationale governing his policy in the first year was that "power can only be kept by educating the masses . . . , only a high level of public education could make possible a conscious governing-by-the-people—which should embrace large masses."

In this report the new administrative forms were detailed. The church was disestablished and religion was eliminated from the curriculum. The private ownership of schools was abolished and all power was vested at the local level in the newly created units of government, the volosts. Only the Unified Workers' School existed at the elementary level and it was based upon a continuous grade or "ladder" system. The organization of the schools into the divisions of lower primary, primary, upper primary, progymnasia, and gymnasia was radically simplified. Two types of schools were established at the secondary level, which were equal in accessibility and social standing. On the one hand were language-oriented "cultural" schools, and on the other were nonlanguage "technical" schools. Specialization before the age of sixteen was prohibited. These secondary schools were eight-year schools, organized into two four-year periods. In addition, fees were abolished, spelling was reformed in the direction of phonetic improvement, and a hot-lunch program was instituted.

Further reforms took place in teacher training, introducing a dual system, with one-year normal schools for the training of elementary teachers and with teachers' institutes for the training of the higher elementary teachers. The universities were granted autonomy; new departments and even whole faculties were added. And, significantly, textbook control was implemented. This was done ostensibly because of the need to revise those books "that inculcated in the minds of the young generation the supremacy of the Tsar of All the Russias." [5]

All of these provisions were of an administrative nature. It yet remained for the spirit to be breathed into the new body. At this stage we can discern the first struggles to expound a coherent and satisfactory theory of education, and for the next few years the ideological and philosophical phase of the revolution occurred.

THE SEARCH FOR AIMS IN
SOVIET EDUCATION

In his first report Lunacharski gave the leading principles of Soviet education. He saw the primary basis of the school resting upon labor and he reported that "The labor character of the school consists in the fact that labor, pedagogical as well as, in particular, productive labor, will be made the basis of teaching." [6] However, the ideological development of the new school did not proceed along any clear path. It is easy to appreciate the enormous difficulties that lay in the way of formulating, from the beginning, a completely new educational policy. On the one hand there was the strong reaction against the conformity produced by the old regime and on the other there was a pressing need to forge a new sort of group solidarity that would hold together the badly fractured society. The result was that much of the early theorizing about education was confused and at times contradictory.

The clearest feature of this theorizing was the unity of belief in the inherent uselessness of the old type of education. In a paper read to the First All-Russian Congress of Teacher-Internationalists on June 2, 1918, Lepeshinski stated that the school had been destroyed as a servant of the ruling classes, and he sought to justify the historicity of the process. The schools were destroyed, not by a group of individuals, "but by the elemental force of life itself. History had paved the way for such a destruction, and it had become a pressing necessity of the present revolutionary period." He also strongly denounced the link between the ruling classes and the church in fostering this servitude, and gave this as the reason for removing education from church control. The new school, he said, should be a place "from which religious services and teachings are absolutely barred." In this speech he gave further details of the nature of the Soviet school; it must be

compulsory and accessible to all, regardless of sex and social distinctions; it must be a school where tuition, books, and so on are free; and lastly, we conceive of the school as a labour unit. The school must be homogeneous in the sense that it is of uniform type, with a definite minimum amount of instruction—in the sense of uniformity of aims and problems grouped between two chief centres of gravitation—and in the producing of an harmonious individual with regard to his social development; and finally, in the sense of establishing an organized connection between the various school grades and unimpeded promotion of students from lower grades to higher.[7]

In this paper Lepeshinski went on to elaborate the features of the new school. In all, six features can be distinguished:

1. The school must produce an early fusion of productive labor and academic instruction.

2. It must aim at all-round development for modern society, that is, polytechnical education.

3. Manual labor must be an integral part of school life.

4. The school should be a productive commune, both producing and consuming, based upon the principles of school autonomy and collective self-determination in the process of mental and manual labor.

5. The widest possible possibilities must be offered for the full play and development of creative forces—self-activity, creative and artistic activity.

6. Character development must proceed in accordance with bringing the child up as a "social creature," and "to produce an understanding of social labor: first, at the present time, then, labor in past history, and last, labor's problems in the near future."

The bias toward the development of the child as a "social creature" is evident in some pronouncements of the same period by Lunacharski. In a document entitled the *Self-education of the Workers* he pointed out that the fundamental struggle of socialist and proletarian culture "is one for an ideal: that of the culture of brotherhood and complete freedom; of victory over the individualism which cripples human beings; and of a communal life based not on compulsion and the need of man to herd together for mere self-preservation, as it was in the past, but on a free and natural merging of personalities into superpersonal entities."

In the same document he elaborated and attempted to justify the six principles upon which the new schools of Russia were to be based. All of these six principles rested upon the notion of the school as a "collective" of some sort, and it is clear that in this regard the thinkers had worked from the premise that the best way either to prepare for a given society or to reconstruct through the school to a desired form of society is to make the school a miniature replica of that society. Hence the achievement of the truly socialist state would be had, in part, by organizing the schools on a collective, socialistic basis. To this end, then, the schools were to have a "collective" character, and this character would be displayed in such things as the production and consumption of group needs. To secure this on some sort of moral basis, an appeal to the necessary historicity of the movement was made, and for this purpose the history of the workers' struggles was used.

Beyond these aims there were certain negative forces shaping the new type of school. These came from the belief that the old schools were necessarily designed to help perpetuate a stratified society. Lunacharski argued that the new type of school "cannot, in any way, resemble that which the ruling class had organized for the 'inferior' working people. In order to destroy this 'class' education we have to adopt the principles of 'one standard of education for all' without any special privileges for anyone." Consequently the old type of school was, of necessity, rejected. In this way, the reconstructionists of the time had to search around for a new principle upon which to base their educational activities.

The chief bases of this line of reasoning were, of course, the generalizations drawn from a study of the division of education. The fact that one class habitually favored one type of education, and that the lower classes, when they received any education at all, tended to get a vocational type, gave rise to the belief that therefore these two types of education were antithetical, and that an academic cultural type of education was inimical to the interests of the working class. There was an emphatic rejection of the bourgeois view of what was good for the workers. In this way Lunacharski,

along with the other architects of the form of Soviet education, for the next decade allowed himself to be forced into
constructing what was to prove a difficult task—a unified,
integral educational plan that would provide for the truly
socialist society; through their reasoning they set artificial
obstacles in their way.

In reasoning this way the architects of education made two
fundamental errors. In making them, they removed from
their armory what could otherwise have proved to be valuable weapons in the fight to improve education in general
and to consolidate the nation in respect to the outside world.
In this first instance, they were not sufficiently versed in the
historical nature of the movement. Rather free with the notion that their form of socialism was determined by historical
necessity, they unfortunately allowed this sort of pseudo-
moral justification to become no more than a glib catch
phrase, obscuring their own perception of the problem. For
it is clear that the progress of education in Russia was already
rapidly breaking down class distinctions. Already the bourgeoisie and the workers were entering into higher education,
and it had long before become one of the proud boasts of the
peasants and workers that they could, through application
and industry, achieve the highest forms of education. Makarenko himself, born into the working class, had achieved no
mean distinction under the old regime. It is true, however,
that the system was vicious and allowed only the most in-
telligent and determined to filter through.

The second error was the assumption that a dual form of
education was necessarily a part of the class system. A causal
relationship was assumed but never really investigated.
Rather, by the very speeches of Lunacharski and others, it is
clear that much of the educational program rested on an
emotional reaction, and not on any clear logico-historical
analysis of the problem. While it is relatively easy to appreciate the argument that the revolution was necessary in order
to speed up the process of mass education, it is not at all clear

that the new order must reject every premise of the old simply because the old order made use of them. And the denial
of the bourgeois values was not in the interests of immediate
reform, as subsequent events were to prove. The hyper-emo-
tionality of the reaction is shown by the fact that the Bolsheviks had seized on the industrial doctrine of Marx and were
bent on implementing it in what was still basically an agricultural form of economy and society.

THE CONFLICT BETWEEN SOVIET
COMMUNISM AND FAMILY LIFE

The nobility and gentry had been disposed of by relatively
simple and direct means—either execution or the threat of
it, which caused them to flee the country in large numbers.
There remained, for the time, little resistance from this direction. What resistance the nobility could offer in the form
of the White Russian counterrevolution was already proving
ineffectual since the Western Allies had lost their enthusiasm
for fighting after the general armistice had been signed. The
peasants, for their part, saw little point in rallying to the support of the squires, insofar as the peasants by supporting
them would lose their rights to squatting on the squires'
land. The major threat, in the eyes of the Bolsheviks, was
from the bourgeoisie, chiefly the *petite bourgeosie*. It was
they who, like a vast corrosive, infiltrated all areas of society
and, with the doctrines of self-help and free enterprise, destroyed the formation of a social cement that would bind together the workers of society into a united, solidaristic common purpose.

The new school, then, was as much directed against the
merchant classes as against the nobility. Hence, "the motto
of the new school must be: 'to live is to work.' We must
therefore take [this] as the starting point of our pedagogical
system, as the chief subject of our teaching, aiming at the
increase of technical knowledge. Our students must feel

themselves part and parcel of the work of the community.
... We must never lose sight of the fact that the chief aim of
education is the knowledge of the various forms of human
culture, which, in its turn, includes all forms of mental and
manual activity." [8]

In their enthusiastic, overzealous drive for the creation of
a socialist utopia, the Bolshevik educators went in for even
greater excesses of fancy. Not content with attempting to
destroy the bourgeoisie by a new form of worker-education,
they fancied that they would have to attack its social roots as
well. Already the family had been singled out as the prime
bourgeois institution, being considered antithetical to the
attainment of true socialist society. Lunacharski was emphatic that the "Woman must cease to be enslaved by the
proletarian kitchen and the proletarian nursery." [9] Lilina,
the head of the Petrograd Education Department, was even
more vehement in her attack during the Educational Conference in Petrograd in 1918. She declared that

We must exempt children from the pernicious influence of the
family. We have to take account of every child, we candidly say
that we must nationalize them. From the first days of their life
they will be under the beneficial influence of communistic kin-
dergartens and schools. Here they shall assume the ABC of Communism. Here they shall grow up as real Communists. Our practical problem is to compel mothers to hand over their children
to the Soviet Government. [10]

Lunacharski was more reserved in his polemic, but nevertheless he too afirmed his belief that

the attention paid to child welfare and the education of the
young in connection with the organization of proletarian elementary schools will lead to the transformation of working-class
family life. [11]

This program was, of course, never really implemented. As
the work of Makarenko will show, the government was unable to handle effectively the war orphans, let alone other

problems. Nevertheless, the desire to communize life remained strong, and during this period a variety of decrees and resolutions were produced to help weaken the bonds of family life. One of the best single accounts of this movement may be found in the text of the original family law of the Russian Soviet Republic, especially in the *Code of Laws Concerning the Civil Registration of Deaths, Births and Marriages* of October 17, 1918.[12] The stress upon the child is clear in Article 153, for example, which states that "Parental rights are exercised exclusively for the benefit of the children. In case of abuse the court is entitled to deprive the parents of their rights."

The strength of the marriage union was weakened by two further actions: religion was subordinated to the state, at least in theory, by the promulgation of the *Decree on the Introduction of Divorce,* December 19, 1917, and by the compulsory civil registration of marriages requirement of December 20, 1917. By this decree divorce became a simple matter of both parties petitioning for annulment of the marriage, without having to state the grounds. That is, the mere fact of mutual petition was reason enough for the dissolution of marriage.[13] The situation was made even more simple with the legalization of abortion on November 18, 1920, in which the Soviet government decided that it would "permit such operations to be performed freely and without charge in Soviet hospitals, where conditions are assured of minimizing the harm of the operation." [14]

Already, as this sort of legislation indicates, the Soviet government was seeking to transform the society. There is some evidence to suggest that this action was based upon a genuine conviction of the need for such utilitarianism. The problem, however, apart from the moral aspects, was complicated by the fact that Marxism offered no clear-cut set of directions on the procedures to be implemented in educational enterprise or reform. Marxism scarcely offered an educational theory at all. This was one of the problems of Soviet educators. For the next fifteen years it was to be the chief one with which they grappled.

THE DILEMMA OF SOVIET EDUCATION

This failure of educational direction was felt as early as 1918. The pronounced reaction against the old type of school was in large part emotional. Thus, at the same time that he was expounding the ideological basis of the new school, Lepeshinski was also proclaiming another doctrine: that the new school required a great deal of experiment. Accordingly, in the paper that he read at the First All-Russian Congress of Teacher-Internationalists on June 2, 1918, he affirmed the need for an experimental basis to socialist education. He said that

What is most needed is not merely world propaganda, but deeds. With this object the Commissariat of Education is organizing experimental schools. It would be an error to assume that here, in the capitals, there is a tendency to introduce bureaucratic methods in the management of schools. We wish to impose nothing upon the people, and when we draw up certain plans, it is chiefly because the population itself, in the person of the organs of local soviet administration units, requires from us a general outline and suggestions.[15]

The contradictions in this doctrine become evident rather quickly, and attest not so much to sheer casuistry as to a genuine confusion in the minds of the planners. At the same conference four days later on June 6 was issued, under the imprimatur of Lunacharski, the *Declaration of the Principles of the Socialist School*.[16] Although in the form of fourteen statements, there are six principles involved. These are:

  1. Socialism is the maximum imaginable realization for our epoch in the collective life of humanity, of an intelligently directed coordination of labor—mental, physical, organizing, and executive.

2. The best possible system is a free, uniform, compulsory, and secular school based upon self-reliance and self-activity, which passes each individual through a complete cycle of knowledge.

3. The school must be a laboratory for the preparation of those social forms which are most appropriate for the contemporary cultural epoch; the struggle for existence becomes changed into an organized cooperation for making human nature follow the commands of man and for the attainment of new truths.

4. The school must be based on selection by intellectual ability.

5. The bourgeois tradition is destroyed by polytechnization, that is, the unification of the mental and manual.

6. The state becomes no longer omnipotent and the subjugator of society but is more simple and more dignified: that is, it becomes a protector.

Already the fundamental dilemma is apparent: to foist nothing on the people and yet to ensure the continued development of the socialist school and the emergence of the socialist society. It often seems that after the initial period of collective solidarity that characterizes revolutions of this sort there is a marked tendency for the peoples to fall apart. Consequently, a period of the most vigorous application of centralized control is often the only way to prevent this. In Makarenko's writings this is most vividly demonstrated. Thus it seems that for one form of utilitarianism another is substituted, and still by a central authority. As time progresses, the maintenance of the external preconditions becomes more and more the matter of concern, and the original *casus belli* becomes forgotten; in the case of Russia, even the proletarian utilitarianism became replaced, or displaced, by bureaucracy.

The underlying Hegelianism is strikingly apparent in the *Declaration of the Principles of the Socialist School*. It is because the planners worked from certain implicit monist assumptions that they were able to assert that the population itself required these sorts of declarations. And yet at the same time they set about the organization of experimental schools, and the elaboration of further contradictions, or at least incompatibles. Within a week of the conference the first experimental school was announced on June 19, 1918. Its aims were to make biological and sociological studies of children of school age, to study the relationships between physical education and formal education, to experiment along the line of an extensive organization of a vocational school, to make experimental investigation of various other methods of educational work, including social and aesthetic education. Then, on September 1, the Institute for Child Study was announced, with the aims of making a "thorough-going study of all questions connected with prescholastic bringing-up and of creating a staff of trained instructors for the solution of urgent problems of today regarding state, social, universal and free education of children of pre-scholastic age." [17]

The confusion of the educational thought of the period reached a high point with the *Education Act of October 16, 1918*. In its preamble the Act stated that:

The personality shall remain as the highest value in the socialist culture. This personality, however, can develop its inclinations in all possible luxury only in a harmonious society of equals. We, the government, do not forget the right of an individual to his own peculiar development. It is not necessary for us to cut short a personality, to cheat it, to cast it into iron moulds, because the stability of the socialist community is based not on the uniformity of the barracks, not on artificial drill, not on religious and aesthetic deceptions, but on an actual solidarity of interests.[18]

Thus they raised the problem of the natural uncoerced coalescence of diverse wills into a cultural unity. The problem is how to guarantee a genuine "solidarity of interests" that will also be capable of acting as a basis for action. It also raises the problem of the treatment of the "peculiar" developments that some individuals may possibly exhibit.

By the end of 1918, within a scarce year of the assumption of power, the Bolsheviks had proceeded to two major tasks, and had at least made a definite statement on both of them. They had laid down the lines of the new system of education, and they had attempted the delineation of educational policy and theory. It seems reasonably certain that a considerable amount of development and struggle would inevitably ensue from the very nature of the haziness and generality of their educational aims before a distinct, definitive educational theory could be produced. To complicate the issue, the actual social ideals which education sought to implement also went through a period of change, indecision, and debate, so that the determination of educational aims and policy often followed an erratic path in attempting to relate itself to a constantly changing ideal.

The following fifteen years formed the chief period through which the most complex of the struggles in education were waged. In accordance with the original Communist ideal, education should be able to be identified as a single enterprise, characterized by a set of related, integral purposes, techniques, methods, and predictable outcomes capable of instrumental use in the attainment of the perfect socialist society. However, such a clear delineation was not present, and in the immediate postrevolutionary years the attempts to formulate such an ideal were many.

Even the principles laid down were themselves confusing and obtained through deductive reasoning from certain idealistic premises. No one could suggest specific educational methods and procedures, nor was there any acceptable psychology of education. What had to take place, therefore, was an inauguration of a vast flurry of experiment, along with a burst of feverish activity and exploration of any and every possibility that could be suggested. What was more difficult was the fact that the Marxian basis of society with respect to its application in nonindustrial Russia had not been derived empirically, but was simply a deductive affair from what in the first place had been highly controversial and debatable principles. One of the dangers that rose like a dragon in the path was the possibility that the theory could be unworkable and, as a corollary, that it would admit of no particular educational form to serve it. This would mean that either the theory would have to change as practice adduced new evidence and principles, or the practice would become increasingly divorced from the ideology, and thus fail to work for its stated goals. What resulted, in effect, was for both things to happen, and in the course of the period between the wars this fascinating social drama worked itself out.

Throughout this period, Russia was fighting a series of counterrevolutionary battles that drew to a close in a final combat with the Poles. In the Treaty of Riga, on March 18, 1921, Russia found herself at peace in Europe for the first time since 1914. By the end of 1921 the country badly needed respite. Already industry was severely reduced, and Pares estimated it at fifteen per cent of its immediate prewar capacity.[19] The farms had become depleted, the country was facing a severe famine, the peasants were uncooperative and in general completely hostile to the urban masses, the country was restless with the vast numbers of displaced persons. In an attempt to straighten out the chaos and to get the new social scheme afloat, a halt was called and the New Economic Policy was inaugurated. Foreign loans, ironically enough, were sought to provide working capital, and a return to partial free enterprise was decreed. This period saw the commencement of the second phase of Soviet educational policy.

MAKARENKO'S ROLE IN THE RESOLUTION
OF THE DILEMMA

Of all of the educators who attempted to help resolve the particular problems of education in this period, none achieved more success than did Makarenko. The solution of the problems was sought in a piecemeal and uncoordinated way, and for quite a while Makarenko remained obscure while other names were prominent. Thus in the early history of Soviet education names like Blonski, Shul'gin, and Pinkevitch are prominent in the literature. But in the final analysis their contributions fade compared to that of Makarenko. For one thing, Makarenko sought to grapple with the whole problem and not with an isolated aspect. For another, Makarenko worked with an unusual group—war orphans—and in doing this he tested the theory and practice to its fullest by its application to marginal groups. In a sense, he had ideal "laboratory animals." Having neither parents nor previous society to struggle with, he could really put his theories into practice without compromise.

In the history of Soviet education, from around this period on, several problems become prominent, of which at least five can be distinguished. These are the problems of providing a true labor basis to education and at the same time keeping it education; of forming collective groups that have a genuine solidarity of interest and are at the same time not antithetical to the wider purposes of collective society; of the resolution of individuality in group life; of the persistence of a traditional morality especially as it is displayed in such things as religion and familial practices; and finally of keeping experiment subordinate to already postulated outcomes. If nothing else, the Soviet educators of the time had to conceptualize these problems so that they bore a meaningful relationship to each other. Then, if they were to be successfully realized in practice, they had to be worked out in their causal relationships so that they would admit of control and educational implementation.

It is the unique and especial contribution of Makarenko that he did, at least to Soviet satisfaction, achieve just this. He was able to decide which of these problems were basic and which were derived. And he attempted to seek the manner of their derivation. Makarenko realized that the collective and labor bases of Soviet education were the fundamental assumptions upon which everything else was based. Yet he also knew that they lacked both a psychology and a rational justification. As yet Soviet educational theory was an untried blueprint; the ideas still lacked real forms. The absence of precise knowledge of how these ideas would work out in practice meant that they were still unpredictable. Makarenko wanted to test the application of every educational idea so thoroughly that it could become a carefully and precisely controlled process leading to a definite and known outcome.

Further problems arose from this, and Makarenko sought to deal with them. Experiment then became for him, not simply a thirst for truth, whatever that may be, but a search for the techniques of controlling processes. Experiment lacked the glamorous overtones that it has achieved in the West and became instead a deliberate process of social engineering. Interfering with the successful achievement of the desired educational purposes was a host of things that continually threw the educator off balance. The whole of inherited traditional morality and ethics did this. While party decrees might officially abolish religion and, later, even God himself, as well as marriage and the family, yet it remained then, as it remains now, only too true that the only real change is one of behavior. Thus Makarenko saw the need to develop a new morality and a new ethics to replace the old ones, and to develop them in such a way that they would assist in and not interfere with the attainment of a new society.

Makarenko did not, of course, begin with these solutions. On the contrary, he ended with them. In the beginning he was conscious, but only vaguely, of what he was up against, and he had to spend many painful years in simply isolating the problems with which he was dealing. The solutions came as slowly. His whole life was a constant dialectic struggle with these problems, and it was only after a decade of unremitting work that he began to achieve articulation of thought and predictability of outcome. And that is the substance of his educational writings—the gradual dialectic unfolding of his thoughts, his actions, and his results as he worked toward the achievement of the Soviet utopia.

CHAPTER 4

THE BESPRIZORNIKI: A CHALLENGE TO SOVIET EDUCATION

THE SPECIFIC EDUCATIONAL PROBLEM

In the previous chapter it was pointed out that among Maka-renko's contributions to the development of Soviet education was the fact that he worked with marginal groups, the war orphans, and thus tested the developing Soviet educational theory and practice to its fullest extent. The challenge to any system of human behavior is always greatest when it is being tried out in the limiting situations, for it is here that breakdowns and failures are most likely to occur. At the same time one comes closer to the ideal conditions for testing a blueprint (as is exemplified, for example, in Plato's *Republic*). Normal social groups are always more resilient and adaptive in their behavior, hence they resist the blueprinted role; to a larger extent than marginal groups they can adapt their behavior to conform to changes in the environment. This adaptability also makes for difficulty of control and interpretation. Contrariwise, normal social groups can often adapt a new theory and practice to their own practices, modifying and changing the notions being experimented with. In the marginal group, however, this change and modification will show up more clearly the faults and deficiencies in the theory being practiced, point out any inconsistencies, locate
46

places where breakdown is most likely to occur, and direct the course of future action.

After World War I there existed for the Bolsheviks many marginal groups that posed problems for the development of Soviet society: displaced persons, the kulaks whom the Bolsheviks dispossessed, the economically ruined middle class, demobilized soldiers, the White Russians—the group is large. Figuring prominently among them was the vast number of children orphaned by the war. To describe these children (called in Russian the *besprizorniki;* singular, *besprizornik*) as war orphans drastically oversimplifies the problem. Nevertheless, for an introduction to the problem it is best to begin with such a general description.

The situation that existed is difficult for English-speaking readers to imagine. Neither England nor her dominions nor the United States suffered the depredations of great armies battling across the countryside, the devastation and occupation of their cities, and the fantastic loss of morale that these events occasioned. The whole of eastern Europe did suffer in this way and the dislocation of normal life was complete. Families were destroyed, homes completely demolished. Many millions of family groups were shattered beyond hope of any future reunion. And along with the war went a wholesale destruction of traditional values. Crime rose alarmingly and the brutalization of human life and values came to be considered usual if not normal. Children suffered terribly in these events and the rise of juvenile crime was appalling.

Statistics on these problems are difficult to obtain and, even though they vary enormously, the most conservative estimates are still huge enough to show that the social disaster was of first magnitude. The official Russian estimates of homeless children were given by Epshtein. He recorded that "In 1922 the total number of Besprizorniki and children, devoid of any means of existence, was calculated at approximately 7,000,000." [1] Allied to the numerical size of the problem was the increasingly ominous shadow of epidemic disease and famine. That something had to be done with these children was apparent. An English observer, Beatrice King, reported the conditions as she saw them at first hand and there is no doubt that her judgment was accurate when she stated that "It is doubtful whether any civilized country was ever faced with the problem of child and adolescent delinquency on so vast a scale and in so acute a form as was Soviet Russia in 1920 and the years following." [2]

The only possibility open to these children, most of them crowded into the slums of the larger cities and towns, was a life of crime. The range of experiences that they encountered in their lives beggared description. Makarenko attempted to describe them, and some of his works are particularly powerful in their analyses of the lives of these children. As the conditions of life became more settled and the immediate military actions stopped, the picture of the extent of the social problem posed by these children became clear. Soviet officials were prompted into making almost disasterwide measures of relief and in the years 1920 and 1921 activities on a national scale were begun to resettle these children into more normal conditions.

Already there was an insurmountable problem in the way. What were the normal conditions that these children were to be brought under? The family had been denounced as a bourgeois institution, inimical to the development of a true Soviet mentality and character, yet at the same time the ideal form of Soviet society remained just that—an ideal. Russia was still socially organized in family groups. To complicate the issue still further, there was no previous pattern to follow: the realization of the ideal had yet to be achieved. Clearly the problem had to be tackled without waiting till an intellectualization of the process had occurred. The pressing need was for action—action designed to remove these children from the streets, from lodging in a host of transient places, from following lives of the utmost viciousness and depravity.

The Soviet government therefore undertook what it called "first aid." Only the most elementary needs could be satisfied on a mass scale, and every possible form of shelter was mobilized: old army barracks, requisitioned church buildings and noble estates, farmhouses, hotels, dining rooms and lodgings—whatever was capable of acting as temporary shelters. A great variety of authorities tackled the problems —the Society of Friends of Children with its two million members, the Institute of Children's Inspectors, the state, the Commission on Juveniles, and a miscellany of children's homes, communes, colonies, and craft schools.[3] There was, however, no over-all organized plan for the rehabilitation of these children, and many of the institutions were run by people completely inexperienced in the education of displaced children.

There was a surprising dearth of theoretical guidance to assist the field workers. Marxist ideology had removed traditional psychology as a useful instrument in effecting some educational purposes, just as it had removed the traditional social form of the family as a goal. Instead, there were only a few hazy principles to act as guides; for example, a belief that the "depravity" of the criminal is the result of economic exploitation, that men desire to act harmoniously together for the common good, and so on. It became small wonder that these children continued to pose a problem and, despite the claim that they were greatly reduced in numbers within a few years, a decade later they still occupied the attention of the government. Writing in the *Great Soviet Encyclopedia* in 1927 Epshtein recorded that "Besprizorniki still represent a great social evil. In the USSR there are still about 334,500 such children and juveniles, distributed as follows: about 300,000 in the RSFSR, about 23,000 in the Ukrainian SSR, about 5,000 in the Byelorussian SSR, about 5,750 in the ZSFSR and about 750 in the Turkemenian SSR."[4]

These besprizorniki created yet another problem. Their treatment would subject the new Soviet system to a trial of strength. Both within and without the country the critics were watching for mistakes. In a sense the new Soviet system, which many had condemned before it had had a fair trial, would be judged by the manner in which it dealt with these children. At the same time there were sincere, genuine humanitarian motives inspiring the government to work. The revolution was still in its romantic, generous stage and the desire to improve the lot of the oppressed victims of "capitalist exploitation" was strong. The Marxist doctrine, like a proud flag, was still being flown high at the masthead of the new republic. The economic location of all problems meant that the institution of public ownership of wealth would of itself remove the social difficulties, according to the new doctrine. There is no doubt that at the time the besprizorniki were considered a problem to be dealt with, they were considered chiefly in terms of being simply a symptom of economic malaise and that they would disappear spontaneously once the economic troubles of the country were removed. Practical steps were needed, and these were forthcoming. Attempts to make these children economically self-supporting by providing them with trades and occupations and placing them in suitable jobs was considered to be part of the program. What was lacking was a thoroughgoing theory of their rehabilitation and a coordination of effort. Gradually, as the twenties progressed, the theory was extracted from the many attempts at reform and the machinery for the implementation of the theory became smoothly organized.

THE CONNOTATION OF THE TERM
"BESPRIZORNIKI"

Strictly translated, the word "besprizornik" means a homeless or neglected child. At times it has been translated as "delinquent," but this is not a felicitous rendition at all. Other frequent translations are "waif" or "stray," but these also lack precision. In attempting to give the flavor of the term, it is true to say that it can include all of these aspects—delinquent, waif, stray—although it does not necessarily include them. The danger is in using it as a strict translation of any one of these words. A further problem is that the word gradually changed its meaning in the Soviet Union during the twenties, especially as the new social system began to give new meaning to old terms in the light of the new ideology.

In Western society children are considered to be delinquent when they fail to live up to certain socially established expectations of behavior; inability to reach such norms is regarded as psychological failure rather than as evidence of criminal intent. Generally, as a correlative of that, the home and family life, duly located in a community setting, is regarded as the normal milieu of the child and as the proper place where these norms are presented and where training in meeting them takes place. Thus delinquency is almost always considered to be due to a breakdown in family and group life, and suggestions for cure always involve a change in the pattern of family living. Behind the whole concept there stands the wider one—that the community at large provides the over-all norms and expectations with the implicit assumption that the individual can operate felicitously only within this pattern of norms and expectations.

The besprizorniki were children who, initially, had little family life, who grew up beyond any system of norms and expectations learned within the context of the family, and who were therefore unable to operate in such terms. In 1926, Makarenko went to an institution in Kuryazh to inspect its possibilities for inclusion in his program of work. Despite the fact that the children in this institution had been there for some time, amounting to several years, they had not yet been brought under any form of control. The director of the institution admitted his inability to deal with the problem. Makarenko describes them:

We went into the dormitory. On dirty, broken bedsteads, on heaps of formless rags, sat waifs, real waifs, in all their glory, huddling under similar rags for warmth. By a dilapidated stove two boys were chopping up a board, evidently recently painted yellow. Filth lay about in the corners, and even in the spaces between the beds.[5]

These children were so completely devoid of norms that they were unable to use eating utensils, even spoons, with any degree of certainty, and were completely covered with vermin. Before they could be dealt with, Makarenko had to shave their heads, burn their clothes and bedding, and disinfect them. Needless to add, many of them were barely literate, if at all, and their habits were not developed enough to include those of work. The basic personality characteristic that they displayed was, to use a term of Leites, "affectlessness." [6] They were not in revolt against anything particularly, nor had they transgressed any particular social norms. They were ignorant of norms, and their experiences of society were such that they lived apart from it. They could not be considered to be deviates because such a concept has implicit within it the notion that the deviant personality has already had incorporated within it the requisite norms and expectations for successful living within that society, and that deviant behavior is that which departs from these norms.

Nevertheless, in relation to the society at large, of which these people were members, albeit unknowingly, they were certainly deviant with respect to their behavior. And as the behavior of the besprizorniki affected that of the rest of the society in no little measure, it was clear that they had to be brought under some form of control. The problem, as Makarenko saw at the outset, was certainly not that of reform. There was nothing to reform. Makarenko stated the problem quite simply "So we have to find new methods for the creation of the new man." [7] These young people had, from the beginning, to be *formed,* their personality, character, intellect had to be moulded and shaped according to some pattern.

And the pattern Makarenko chose was his still unclear notion of the new socialist man.

THE IDEALISTIC CONSTRUCTION OF THE MEANING OF BESPRIZORNIK

Makarenko was not the only person concerned with the construction of the new Soviet man or the formation of the besprizorniki. The subject received considerable attention from a number of sources, although it is true that Makarenko's work was never eclipsed by any other worker. In defining the term besprizornik, certain ideological dimensions were distinguished in the middle twenties, and they are given authoritative pronouncement by Professor A. Zalkind in the 1927 edition of the *Great Soviet Encyclopedia*. In his article "Besprizornost' " he takes up three issues: the causes, the psychology, and the re-education of besprizorniki.[8]

The causes of children becoming besprizorniki are given as fundamental postulates by Zalkind. There is no argument: they are simply and baldly stated to be exclusively socioeconomic. Thus children who have lost their homes, along with those who live in homes where their parents neglect or ill-use them, come within the general category. Much of the blame Zalkind placed squarely on the Western capitalist powers. Although he admits that similarly neglected children exist in Western countries, he argues, though not very cogently, that they are somehow "different," without attempting any precise analysis of this difference. In the Soviet Union, the civil and imperialistic wars, the foreign blockades and intervention and consequent economic ruin, have all conspired to produce this particular group of children. They are produced by a society which has been so crippled by outside interference, Zalkind states, that the children can no longer be adequately cared for. Thus the environment alone, and its conditioning power, is responsible for the phenomenon.

Implicit in Zalkind's argument are certain developmental assumptions that never become quite consciously stated. This can be seen in his description of the "psychology" of the phenomenon. Because of the early involvement in the brutal struggle of the streets, these children develop inharmoniously, and their personality acquires a set of distinctive traits that mark them off from other children. He distinguishes seven of these "traits," these being:

1. An early development of a deep and acute instinct for self-preservation;

2. A rapid development of the sense organs which often outstrips the growth of the higher "abstract" functions;

3. An excitability and a strongly growing emotional life;

4. An awakening of the sensual elements of sexual life, thus partly disorganizing further normal standard physiological development;

5. The ripening of a set of adventurous aspirations, produced on the one hand by the conditions of street life, and on the other cultivated naturally by the normal development of adventurous inclinations;

6. The appearance of violent behavior, the failure of their social development and the working of instability, explained by the rapidly changing conditions of the street struggle for existence;

7. The development of a need for artificial excitements: narcotics, alcohol, and passion.

An argument of this type poses certain problems for a Communist educator. For a start, the developmental assumptions become very difficult to explicate, insofar as the only real model has been that of past experience which, in the Soviet Union as elsewhere, was specifically capitalistic and predominantly class-oriented. Of course, to deny the existence of individual, inner developmental tendencies means that the whole of human behavior has to be explained in environmental terms. Zalkind did this, and thus was able to find certain positive values in the life of the besprizorniki. For a start, he found that at the very least these children had not been infected with any bourgeois morality. On the contrary, the nature of their life included the necessary seeds of their regeneration. For they had developed quite early the characteristics of the true proletarian fighter for the new socialism: realism, toughness, flexibility, courage, perception, activity, solidarity in group action, and an aversion for the bourgeois way of life.

This points up a contrast in ways of dealing with them. In the bourgeois West, he argued, these children are looked upon as depraved and criminal and therefore their treatment is by means of punitive and penitential methods in prison shelters, correctional institutions, and under other severe conditions. To support his position he analyzed the treatment of these children in England through the years 1919 to 1924 inclusive, although the source of his data is not given. In his account of the children dealt with by the courts, 13,365 were sent to industrial schools, 274 went to jails, 12,788 were placed in reformatories. Further, 25,911 were subjected to corporal punishment and 175,277 were given some form of financial penalty. It is difficult, however, to see how these could be comparable cases.

In the Soviet Union, the different assumptions regarding the creation and treatment of these children led to a totally different means of dealing with them. They were not considered to be criminals, nor were they in need of punitive reformatory treatment. As these children were produced through temporarily disorganized and unsettled conditions, and as they were assumed to be thirsting after wholesome living accommodation and organized independent work, the task was one of providing them with the conditions that would enable them to work at social self-education. Due, of course, to the distinctive set of traits which they had developed, their treatment must take this into account, and these traits must be changed calmly by nonviolent, educative means. Thus, according to this theory re-education depends on cultivating in these children a faith in themselves and in their abilities for reform. To this end the atmosphere of establishments devoted to this cause should consist of a faith between pupil and educator, an intimate rapport born of everyday living together and a close community of interests.

In addition to the assumption that the phenomenon of the besprizorniki was due exclusively to environmental conditions, the further assumption of their thirst for "belongingness" was made. And again the Communist educator got dangerously close to the idea of "normalcy" being that of the bourgeois family. Thus Zalkind considered that these children were disorganized and unsettled in relation to *the society of other children*. But this, if pursued, leads into further difficulties, especially insofar as these children had been enjoying the company of other children—indeed, too much so.

By now it should be clear that a simple one-to-one translation of the word besprizorniki is not possible, certainly with respect to those millions of children immediately after the war. "Delinquency" in some ways suffices, especially in the later years. After the massive shock treatment organized to cope with the problem, the besprizorniki continued to come forward and they were being educated in communes and colonies throughout the thirties. At this time they could scarcely be the same group of war orphans that originally posed the problem. It would, of course, be much truer to speak of the later ones as being more or less delinquents, especially as the family had been reaccepted and many of the children were uncontrollable or in some form of revolt against their families. Thus a shift in the meaning of the word occurred as the composition of the group changed. Nevertheless, the original word and the original psychological and sociological assumptions underlying it remained in Soviet literature during Makarenko's working life, and as he never changed his original view of their nature, or his treatment, it is essential to think of the besprizorniki as being something different from that connoted by the word "delinquent." In view of this, it seems the safest course, having explained the connotation of the word, to leave it untranslated. Thus, in the following pages, where the original Russian word is besprizorniki, it will be retained as that in the English.

MAKARENKO AND THE BESPRIZORNIKI

Whatever his fervent devotion to the ideal of Communism, the Soviet educator faces certain considerable problems by beginning with Marxist dicta. At the time that Makarenko was working this was especially so. The argument presented by Zalkind, for example, runs perilously close to being pure casuistry, and the separation of Marxist ideology from capitalist ideology, and the consequent deduction of practical measures, requires the exercise of a very nice judgment. Makarenko never achieved this felicitous state. Often his original conception of Marxist doctrine was hazy, and very frequently he made interpretations of the doctrine that subjected him to violent criticism, especially in the early "romantic" period of the twenties. During these years Marxist doctrine was still being disputed, and the period of the great reaction and its attendant repression was yet to come. Makarenko certainly accepted some of the widest, most general of the Marxist ideals as fundamental postulates, and he worked unflinchingly to implement them. There is no doubt that part of his problem lay in his lack of intellectual sophistication and academic training. Thus he appeared a provincial rustic in comparison with the more polished and more erudite scholars working at the solution of educational problems. This he no doubt was, from his obviously Ukrainian name—which in Russian is without the honor of grammatical inflection—through to his rough, untutored manners.

Whatever his political persuasions, no real scholar or educational philosopher could get very far with the Marxist dicta on educat on. A vast amount of interpretation, testing, application, anc so on was needed for the construction of a workable practice of education. Naturally, psychology and the social sciences were brought to bear on the solution of the problem, as was the experience of other countries. Thus, during the twenties, in an effort to penetrate the mysteries of true Soviet ecucation, vast testing movements were undertaken, with which the name Blonski is synonymous. The Kilpatrick project method was adapted to the apparent needs of Soviet education, as were the platoon school movement and the Dalton plan Psychological clinics sprang up everywhere, depth psychology and the clinical interview became standard for the investigation of problem children, the "developmental case-history" for each child was a growing fad. Slowly but surely the psychologizing of much of Soviet education was at hand.

Makarenko, however, was not in touch with any of this. Remote in his native Ukraine he worked at the more prosaic task of the daily teaching grind, his mind busy grappling with the thousand and one immediate problems that many teachers face unceasingly. Despite his gold medal at the Poltava Teachers' Institute, he was far from scholarly in his background. On the contrary, Makarenko appeared to be sadly out of touch with the best ideas of the contemporary educational thought. Ignorant of psychology, he took the practical teacher's refuge in ridiculing it. Unable to understand a philosophical treatment of what to him were pressing educational problems, he became derisive of any attempt to analyze educational problems theoretically and instead took an increasing pride in his own "practicality." All of this brought Makarenko into conflict with the opinion prevailing at the higher levels of educational thought, and frequently the laughter was at his expense. Makarenko took his revenge at first with crude caricatures of the psychologists and theoreticians, but in his later writing the caricature changed to merciless satire.

Makarenko accepted certain of the ideals laid down by Zalkind as fundamental to his work. In the first place, he accepted the environmentalist notion of the cause of the phenomenon of the besprizorniki. Secondly, he also accepted the notion that children fundamentally crave belongingness— that inside they seek a normal, regular life of productive work, and that properly stimulated they will accept this as their usual mode of life. As deductions from these assumptions, and also due to his own emotional dispositions, he thoroughly rejected any form of psychology or of the psychologization of education, as psychology was then understood. It is true that he did seek to develop a psychology of education, but it was to be a truly Soviet psychology free of the bourgeois assumptions and pseudoscientific methods that the Communist educators were busy copying from the West. Indeed, in Russia at the time, the whole of the scientific movement in education was known as "pedology," within which came the use of psychology, and it was against the movement as a whole that Makarenko directed his criticism. Makarenko wanted to develop a psychology from the beginning that was indigenous to the Russian people and true to Marxist doctrine. Quite early in his career he rejected any individual psychology and instead worked in the direction of a social psychology. In one sense, his career was the explication of a specifically Marxist social psychology.

Due in part to his rabid adherence to Marxism, and as much to his ignorance of the possibilities of a scientific approach to education, along with a strong trait of ordinary, warm love of humanity, Makarenko quite literally began at the beginning. Almost from the outset he refused to have any measurement or evaluation made of his besprizorniki— no intelligence testing, no attainment testing, no personality diagnosis. His rejection of these scientific methods was in part an intuitive reaction, although he made attempts to ex-

amine his own conscience on his stand. Along with this he
refused to recognize the child's past. When new arrivals came
to his institution they were usually accompanied by a thick
dossier detailing their past, their criminal record, their interview records, and so on. Makarenko refused after a short
time even to open these records and often returned them
with the seals intact. For him each child was a new, fresh
challenge, a challenge to the new Soviet education. Makarenko felt that the child's past was no part of its future and
he adhered strictly to that principle throughout. Nor did
Makarenko ever seek to delve into the past in depth inter-
views under any guise whatever. His view was always directed
toward the future. Thus the children were never encouraged
to talk about the past, but instead the vision of a better world
that they could achieve by their own unremitting group effort was held before them.

In a way these children were simply ethnographic material
—they came without history and so without previous existence. They were to constitute an experimental group par
excellence. As we turn to their story as told by Makarenko,
his remarkable achievements can be seen as the story unfolds.

PART II
THE DEVELOPMENT OF A NEW SOVIET EDUCATION

CHAPTER 5
THE ROAD TO LIFE

INTRODUCTION

Makarenko's greatest single contribution to the literature of education is his remarkable trilogy, *The Road to Life*. By whatever standards a work on education is judged, this must surely rank as great. Even in its translation into English it has the power to evoke emotion, to penetrate to the essence of the situations and problems that Makarenko faced, and to carry the reader effortlessly through the intricate web of problems and crises presented by the task of reclaiming seemingly lost and degenerate lives. Although it is an idealistic reconstruction of the past, it suffers from no overly romantic interpretation. Makarenko is careful to keep the events in their true relations to each other, and, as he writes, he records with the same fidelity his failures and frustrations as well as his successes and joys. Part of the great charm of the book is the honesty with which events are depicted, an honesty that searches out the whole range of human emotion and gives to the work that aura of wholeness and completeness that makes it live. Were this Makarenko's sole work, he would be remembered.

The Road to Life is a reconstruction of the seven years, from September 3, 1920, to September 3, 1927, in which Makarenko labored in the Gorki Colony for besprizorniki

63

near Kharkov. In that time he achieved the remarkable success of turning some hundreds of children whose lives were on the edge of disaster into wholesome, positive people able to move on and to take their places as reputable members of society. In addition, through his devotion to his humble and obscure task, he was able to devise a system that spread throughout the Soviet Union, providing a model for others to follow.

Makarenko, devoted to the Bolshevik cause (although he was never a member of the Communist Party, the honor coming posthumously), became nevertheless extremely dissatisfied with events immediately after the Revolution, especially with the way that the great cause was failing to spread its doctrine. Rather critical of the educational provisions in the region of the Ukraine in which he was teaching, his criticisms reached the ears of the chief of the Provincial Department of Public Education. The chief, as a challenge to Makarenko's sincerity, offered him the task of organizing an institution for besprizorniki. Little could be provided beyond an old, deserted prewar farm used for the housing of juvenile delinquents (maloletnikh prestupnikov) six kilometers from Poltava. Makarenko was given some money, but beyond that he was told that he, the handful of teachers, and the children would all have to shift for themselves.

Shift they did, and with astonishing success. Within a few years the place became a thriving institution called the Maxim Gorki Colony. Early in his life Makarenko had become spellbound by the name of Gorki and adopted him as his hero-figure. When it came time to name his colony, he could do no better than to name it after one of the most influential figures in his life. Gorki was held up as a model to the children themselves, his works becoming popular reading in the colony, and in 1928 Gorki actually came in person to visit them. Gorki was an influence in other ways. In addition to providing a hero-figure for the boys to emulate, he corresponded with Makarenko and took an interest in Makarenko's literary efforts. In an earlier chapter it was mentioned how Makarenko received a severe jolt when Gorki criticized his early efforts. Despite this, Gorki later encouraged Makarenko to write an account of the Gorki Colony. With this inspiration, Makarenko began, in 1925, five years after the establishment of the colony, to write its moving story.

THE STRUCTURE OF *The Road to Life*

The colony moved altogether through three locales: first was the original estate of the old farm for juvenile delinquents, then an abandoned noble estate—Trepke, and finally a badly run-down colony for besprizorniki at Kuryazh near Kharkov. The three volumes of *The Road to Life* cover these three phases, each phase corresponding to a volume. The writing of the trilogy is interesting, for it is written entirely in the first person, as if it were Makarenko's diary, and at times he lapses into what are almost meditative silent soliloquies. After a while it becomes clear that the story is a rationalization of the work actually accomplished—an attempt to put the events in relation and in their proper perspective. In *The Road to Life* Makarenko is working out, dialectically, the practice and theory of his educational work. This explains the trilogy format. Despite his dislike of the psychologists, *The Road to Life* is a psychological study of Makarenko's own mind, it is a psychologization of his thought. Thus the three volumes correspond to the three phases through which he went, both in theory and practice, in the evolution of his method.

In the first volume he was faced with a confused, baffling situation: he was in charge of a group of human flotsam who obeyed no usual rules, who had no predictable responses. Through this he searched for a structure, he attempted to perceive the group and his own relations to it in meaningful terms—terms such that he could begin to control and organize the children and then to direct them to meaningful and purposeful tasks of re-education. This covers a three-year period, and by then Makarenko felt that he had achieved the beginnings of a workable system.

In the second volume, when the mistakes had been made and the children had been subjected to some sort of a system, the colony conveniently moved to a new locale. Not very far away in distance, it was the abandoned noble estate of Trepke. Psychologically, however, it was a significant distance because Makarenko took the children there as an organized group, and this gave its own force in reorienting the outlook of his besprizorniki. In this second volume Makarenko elaborated a rationale to explain the system that was largely derived by empirical means. Trepke represented, symbolically, the union of theory and practice.

One final task remained ahead of Makarenko: the applicability of his system to other groups. He had to move his colony yet a third time, to a run-down home for besprizorniki at Kuryazh, on the outskirts of Poltava. Again the move was greater psychologically than it was in distance. At Kuryazh he proceeded to apply the theory developed on the other group to a totally new one. In this case, the system existed prior to the group and Makarenko wished to see whether he had discovered a universal system that existed independently of the original group from which it evolved. The third volume is a record of his attempts and his experiences with such an application.

Altogether, Makarenko took ten years in the production of this work.[1] Originally begun in 1925, it was not completed until 1935, seven years after he had left the Gorki Colony, and it was first published in its final form in that year. Originally it was titled *Pedagogicheskaya Poema,* which, strictly translated, is *Pedagogical Poem* and, in the interests of a more literary and significant description, became translated as *An Epic of Education.* In the Russian editions it always appears as just that. The translation, however, by Ivy and Tatiana Litvinov, issued by the Moscow Foreign Languages

Publishing House, gives the title as *The Road to Life* (*Putevka v Zhizn'*) and it carries the subtitle of *Pedagogicheskaya Poema.* In general, the more romantic, idealized title is a better description of the book and in Russia it is coming to be called by that title in recent literature.

Whether the correspondence of the three locales of the institutions with the three stages of Makarenko's thought and practice is simply fortunate or is a deliberate attempt to give a coherence to the work is a difficult question to decide. There is no doubt that the story has been carefully and thoroughly sifted to ensure that the fundamental issues are kept clearly before the reader. And Makarenko wanted to keep them clearly before his own mind too. To this end, only the critical issues are recorded, along with sufficient grist to make them digestible. Yet at the same time Makarenko was careful to record his failures and his problems as well. In the end, the problems do not all disappear. On the contrary, many of the problems that he failed to solve were carefully recorded and became the targets of his later work. It seems, from the evidence, that there is something of both his successes and his failures in the work. If his records are accurate, as they appear to be, then there is no gainsaying the achievements within each of the institutions. Each represents a definite step forward in the evolution of his thought and practice. On the other hand, as his own later evidence testifies, he was far from solving the problems that he thought he had solved at each particular stage; the separate volumes are, to a certain extent, oversimplifications of the problems. Nevertheless, the way Makarenko conceived of the problems, the consequent development of a system to solve them, and the elaboration of an explanatory rationale are there as definite achievements and remain eloquent testimony of the man's great accomplishments.

CHAPTER 6

THE SEARCH FOR MEANING

THE BEGINNINGS OF THE GORKI COLONY

At the time that Makarenko took over the Gorki Colony the social and political organization of Soviet life was far from settled. The army was still acting as a police force and occasionally the scene of action between warring military groups was near the colony. The many small actions between the Bolsheviks and their numerous opponents had not drawn to a close. The distribution of power among the various civil authorities was not yet effective, nor had the chains of command been established. It was not clear, for instance, under whose real authority the Gorki Colony was to come. The teachers were supplied by the local education authority, and it was the chief of the Provincial Education Department who appointed Makarenko. Apart from the buildings and lands, which were in hopeless order, and a small sum of money, there was little more the chief could give Makarenko beyond his blessing. Certainly he had no educational advice to offer to the naïve Anton. When Makarenko desired advice on how to go about his task, being apprehensive about failure, he asked of the consequences. There could be no muddle, the chief replied:

"You and your 'make-a-muddle'! What are you driving at? D'you think I don't understand? Muddle or no muddle, the work's got

68

to be done. We'll have to judge by results. The main thing isn't just a colony for juvenile delinquents, but—you know!—er . . . social re-education. We've got to create the new man, you know —our sort of man. *That's* your job! Anyhow, we've all got to learn, and you'll learn. I like the way you said to my face: 'I don't know!' Very well, then!" *

It was in this spirit that Makarenko set out to take over one of the colonies that were established to handle the millions of children who had been orphaned by the war.

The plant itself was in a very poor state. The members had run away in 1917 and the local peasants had set about the task of dismantling and carting away every possible item of use. The buildings were arranged in a symmetrical square, constructed of brick and situated in the middle of a 40-hectare (98.8 acres) clearing in a pine forest four miles from Poltava. So efficient had the peasants been in their looting that they had carefully removed windows from the spaces in the wall, frames and all, and with the greatest care had even dug up the fruit trees for replanting. As Makarenko reported, "there was not the slightest indication of a spirit of vandalism!" (I, 29).

Within a day or two his staff arrived and they were, to say the least, as inexperienced and nonplused as he was. The chief staff member was an old army guardsman, Kalina Ivanovitch Serdyuk, who came as supply manager but who before long acted as general factotum. In addition to Kalina there were two women teachers: Ekaterina Grigoryevna, a seasoned pedagogue, and Lydia Petrovna, a young girl scarcely out of school herself. It was not until several months later, on December 4, Makarenko records, that the first six charges arrived,

* Makarenko, A. S., *The Road to Life*, Foreign Languages Publishing House, Moscow, 1955, vol. I, pp. 26–27. Quotations in this chapter all come from this edition, and the volume number and pages are given in parentheses at the end of the quoted material. Transliterated Russian words, given within the text in parentheses, were taken from the *Pedagogicheskaya Poema* in the *Sochineniya v Semi Tomakh*, given in the bibliography.

presenting me with a fantastic packet bearing five huge seals. This packet contained their "records." Four of them had been sent to us for housebreaking while bearing arms. These were about eighteen years old. The other two, who were a little younger, had been accused of theft (I, 36).

The start was hardly promising. The six simply ignored Makarenko and the staff. They kept going off to the town at night and returning to the colony by day to loaf around. Makarenko, already loath to use any form of compulsion or coercion, kept hoping that the boys would become attracted to the staff and begin to evince interest in working, both at lessons and in the fields. This, however, the boys showed not the slightest desire to do. As the months went by, they continued to be insolent and apathetic to the staff and continued to slip away from the colony on their nocturnal visits to Poltava. For his part, Makarenko was still idealistic, believing that once the boys saw that there were only good intentions present they would naturally and spontaneously seek the guidance of the teachers. The winter wore on and still the six besprizorniki remained coldly indifferent to the staff. All ten of them were in some strange, surrealistic situation, moving among each other as if in an unreal world—or at least in a world in which the rules are vastly different. Makarenko described this, getting to the essence of the situation:

The lonely forest surrounding the colony, the empty shells of our buildings, our dozen camp beds, the axes and spades which were almost our only tools, the half-dozen boys who were in frank opposition not only to our pedagogical system, but to the very principles of human culture itself—all this was as unlike as possible to any scholastic experience any of us had ever had (I, 38).

In that first winter Makarenko sought desperately to find guidance, reading everything and anything pedagogical that he could to help in the task. Already Makarenko's firm resolves had weakened to the point where he had to procure a revolver in order to meet anticipated difficulties, and within six months it seemed that his idealistic resolve was doomed to failure. He was bitter about the inability of the texts on education to give him any direct guidance and from this time forward showed a profound antagonism toward any form of education which stressed psychology.

The first real breakthrough came quite unexpectedly. Makarenko recorded that

The colony was becoming more and more like a den of thieves and cutthroats. The attitude of the boys to their teachers was rapidly crystallising into habitual insolence and frank hooliganism. By now they were bandying dirty stories in front of the women teachers, rudely demanding their dinner, throwing plates about the dining room, making open play with their Finnish knives and inquiring facetiously into the extent of everybody's possessions, with jeering remarks such as: "You never know when that might come in handy!"

They flatly refused to cut down trees for firewood, breaking up the wooden roof of a shed under the nose of Kalina Ivanovitch, joking and laughing good-humouredly the while (I, 42–43).

During this time Makarenko's search for pedagogical guidance had been continuing fruitlessly. He realized that he would "have to wring my own theories out of the sum total of the actual phenomena as displayed in everyday life" (I, 42). He was, in his own words, walking a "pedagogical tightrope" at the time. But still the behavior of the children was as nonconformist as ever, and

one day, the storm broke. I suddenly lost my footing on the tightrope of pedagogical practice. One wintry morning I asked Zadorov to chop some wood for the kitchen stove, receiving the usual cheerfully insolent reply: "Do it thyself! God knows there are plenty of you here!"

It was the first time any of the boys addressed me with the familiar "thou." Desperate with rage and indignation, driven to utter exasperation by the experiences of the previous months, I raised my hand and dealt Zadorov a blow full in the face. I hit him so hard that he lost his balance and fell against the stove. Again I struck him, seizing him by the collar and actually lifting him off his feet. And then I struck him the third time.

. . . .

An iron poker had somehow found its way into my hand. The other five huddled speechless around their beds. . . .

Turning towards them, I rapped with the poker against the foot of one of the beds.

"Either you all go this minute to work in the woods, or you leave the colony, and to hell with you!"

With this I left the room (I, 43–44).

It was from this moment on that the Gorki Colony became established and Makarenko had unconsciously formulated his first principle, a principle that he was to recognize later and to which he gave conscious expression. Zadorov, who was beaten up, was in fact physically larger and stronger than Makarenko and both of them knew this. As the days followed, the boys set to work, and actually began to talk of Makarenko's creed. With that marvellous intuition that guided him through a maze of similar and far more tricky situations, Makarenko was able to seize upon the essential issue in the situation. Zadorov could have easily retaliated, and equally Makarenko could have simply sent the boy back to the Commission for Juveniles as incorrigible rather than beating him. Makarenko was close to the truth when he said that

I didn't do any of this; instead I chose a way which was dangerous for myself, but it was a human, not a bureaucratic way. And after all they do really need our colony. Things are not so simple. And they see how we work for them. They're human beings, too. And this is a most important factor (I, 50).

THE BEGINNINGS OF GROUP SOLIDARITY

Makarenko had struck the spark that set things going. The realization that he had endangered his own job by striking one of them, which was strictly against the law, made a deep impression on these youths. More than anything else they realized that Makarenko was human. Makarenko for his part strove desperately to keep the boys working lest they should begin to slacken off as the event receded into the distance. For the next months Makarenko became engrossed with the problem of finding some principle of keeping the group interested in work.

Meanwhile the colony expanded quickly. In February, 1921, fifteen ragged, infected besprizorniki arrived and the next month another nine came, making a total of thirty boys altogether. The task of providing for this number as well as for the extra staff that arrived became increasingly difficult. The famine was beginning to make its effects felt, and also there was no supply of clothing for the colony. Food consisted solely of a thin millet gruel called "kondyor" and the boys had to wind strips of cloth around their feet as footwear in the bitter winter. Throughout the difficulties of this period Makarenko worked unremittingly, and it was through the obvious devotion to their cause that he gradually began to win over the boys. Once they had been given a shock to get them over their inertia they were able to keep moving. Ever honest with the boys, Makarenko's actions in meeting their needs that winter became the first real bond between them.

Due to the confusion of authority and to the inefficiency of the various public bodies, it was not clear who was to feed the colony. The actions of Makarenko in securing food became rather bold, and at times he came dangerously close to being arrested for improper actions. With the open knowledge of the boys, Makarenko did the rounds of the various supply authorities, getting from each, under various pretexts, a supply of food, chiefly flour. Keeping rigorously to his principle of the primacy of the common good, Makarenko kept no special things for himself. His aim was to develop a consciousness of the primacy of the group, and he saw very early that he had to include himself as one of them. If he kept apart, then the division between leader and led would have destroyed, in his opinion, the effectiveness of his leadership. What Makarenko was seeking, unconsciously, was to realize as efficiently as he could a principle of social psychology—that participatory leadership is more effective in influencing group attitudes and opinions than supervisory leadership.

Very early in the life of the colony Makarenko found cause to make a considerable fuss over an attempted violation of this principle, and this instance showed another of Makarenko's characteristics: whenever he felt that a critical issue had arisen that would influence the future direction of the group life, he made his actions and thoughts as vociferous as possible. In this particular case, Taranets, one of the boys, was anxious to secure Makarenko's favors. Highly impressed with the way that Makarenko wrote official-sounding requisition forms for food and was able to pass them off as genuine at some of the various supply depots, Taranets copied this behavior and began catching fish from the nearby river, making unofficial use during the night of nets belonging to nearby farmers.

One day Taranets brought to Makarenko a plate of cooked fish which, to Taranets' consternation, Makarenko refused to accept. Taranets argued that he had a right to offer the fish—after all he had only borrowed the fishing nets. But Makarenko was adamant, and as loudly as possible he proceeded to explain the basis of his refusal. Having pointed out that Taranets was violating the principle of the unity of the colony, Makarenko launched into a tirade:

"Whose frying pans do you use? Your own? No—everyone's! And the sunflower oil you wheedle out of the cook—whose is that, d'you think? Everyone's of course! And the wood, the stove, the pails? Well—what have you to say to that? I have only to confiscate your *yateri* [the fish], and that would be the end of it. But it's your uncomradely spirit that's worst of all. What if the nets are yours—you have your comrades to think of. . . ."

I accepted the fish, and from that day, everyone took a turn at fishing, and the catch was sent to the kitchen (I, 61).

In this way, Makarenko would dispose of actions which seemed to work against the spirit of the group as a whole. In doing this, of course, there was a fundamental contradiction which Makarenko never fully worked out and which, from the beginning, was to be the cause of the failure of part of his system. Clearly a moral dilemma was involved. Why could Makarenko on the one hand insist on the interrelatedness and group ownership of everything, which carried with it the implicit notion of sharing, and yet on the other hand get flour and other supplies for the colony by faking official-looking orders, thus taking advantage of the chaos in the system of distribution of food? Makarenko himself never raised the issue; if he had, he would have destroyed his own arguments in front of the boys.

In fact, Makarenko never consciously formulated any notion of the complete interrelatedness of the total society of which his boys were a part. He did use, of course, and frequently, such stock phrases as "our glorious system of soviets" and "our great Communist society." Makarenko used these terms as normative rather than descriptive definitions of Soviet society, and all through his work it is clear that it is an ideal future society of which he is constantly talking. Thus he was able to proceed to the formation of a tight in-group structure within his colony which was pursuing, certainly, the road to life; but it was the road to a future ideal life and a life which discounted current society as part of it. Thus, in the early days of his work at the Gorki Colony Makarenko never saw beyond the group itself, and the boys began to develop a group solidarity which chiefly came from considering themselves as a unit isolated from the rest of society, not unlike the gang principle that operates for some street-gang groups.

Gradually the colony began to assume a routine of daily life in which the affairs of ordinary living were carried forward without more than the normal amount of incident that would attend any boys' camp. Makarenko, however, was constantly seeking for issues that he could build up into crises in the life of the group. In the multitude of daily problems there were many possibilities, and Makarenko was astute enough to pick out the really significant ones. Thus he directed his attention at external actions that were able to be perceived by the boys themselves in simple terms. For example, thieving was a frequent target of his attentions, and in 1921, when another of the boys, Burun, had been found to have engaged in a systematic course of stealing, chiefly from the housekeeper, Makarenko worked it up into a full-scale issue.

Burun was a pathetic figure who had belonged to a band of robbers that had been caught and—with the exception of Burun, whose mere seventeen years saved him—had been shot. Nevertheless, Makarenko seized his opportunity and he convened—for the purpose of "trying" Burun—the very first of the "people's courts" to be held in the history of the colony. It was a remarkable affair—thirty besprizorniki assembled to try an "enemy of the Soviet people!" And Makarenko played his part for all it was worth.

Makarenko's description of the scene sounds like something from Hogarth:

In the dormitory, seated on beds and tables, were ranged the ragged and grim-visaged jury. The rays from the oil-lamp lit up the tense faces of the boys, and the pale countenance of Burun, who, with his heavy, awkward frame and thick neck, looked like a typical American gangster.

In firm, indignant tones I described the crime to the boys: to have robbed an old woman, whose only happiness consisted in her wretched possessions, to have robbed one who had shown more affection for the boys than anyone else in the colony, just when she had turned to them for aid—surely anyone capable of this must be, not simply a beast, but a skunk! A man should be able to respect himself, should be strong and proud, and not rob feeble old women of their little all.

Whatever the cause—whether my speech made a great impression, or whether the boys were sufficiently aroused anyhow—Burun became the object of a united and vehement attack (I, 72).

After a frenzy of vehemence, in which suggestions from a beating-up to expulsion from the colony were suggested by the colonists, Burun threw himself on the mercy of the court —which was, in effect, to ask Makarenko to relieve him of what was becoming a considerable disturbance in his life. For Burun, like the others, had never been subjected before to a situation in which his own group condemned him.

Burun appealed to Makarenko, and swore never to steal again. In his oath of loyalty, he included an appeal that became another cardinal principle in Makarenko's method: "Give me any punishment you like, only don't expel me from the colony" (I, 75). Makarenko sensed immediately that threat of expulsion from the colony had great force, and slowly and surely he organized the next issue so that it would hinge on expulsion. He was helped in this because life at that time was most unattractive in the outside world, and the boys were conscious of the security of the place, of its regular meals and of the ease with which they could identify with the hero-ideal of Makarenko. Indeed, as the famine wore on, the colony became a haven, especially as it became self-sufficient in food production.

Makarenko learned through Burun that the boys were beginning to see the colony in a favorable light, compared with the outside world, and he began to make liberal use of threats to expel those who failed to conform to requirements. Further, he was already moving toward a clearer view of what the ideal life was, and at the same time he was becoming more antagonistic toward the outside world of reality. He became ever firmer in his convictions of the value of the in-groupness of the colony and he stopped at nothing to preserve its character. Thus the expulsion of a member was less a matter for qualms than would be the breakdown of the precious, fragile beginnings of group solidarity. It was not long before this issue would be made explicit to the group.

Already the shadow of expulsion had been cast with the threatening of Burun. Makarenko was well aware that he had to precipitate a crisis in order to achieve the next stage. His analysis of the problem was that there was too much self-preoccupation. In his own words,

> During our first year one of our greatest vexations was the perpetual tendency to quarrel among themselves, the appalling weakness of the ties which must exist in any collective, but which in their case broke down every minute over the merest trifles (I, 116).

At the very time that these thoughts were in his mind, the crisis presented itself. The boys had taken to each other with knives in a bitter quarrel.

Makarenko settled the episode of the knives and was able to disperse the group to bed, having confiscated a remarkable assortment of weapons. After the incident, neither he nor the boys said anything about it for a few months, although it still remained a simmering issue. After a few more outbreaks of a minor sort another large fight occurred. Makarenko realized that it was time to precipitate matters; in his own words "... I realized I should have to tighten the screws" (I, 120).

One of the worst offenders was the tragic ill-starred figure of Chobot, who was to remain one of the limits that tested the system and about whom more will be said later. At this stage Chobot had figured prominently in the knife attacks and Makarenko decided to make an example of him. (Although it is easy to be wise after the event, nevertheless in picking Chobot as the scapegoat Makarenko set in process a series of actions that were to culminate for Chobot in his desperate and frightening death, a fact which at once testifies to the grim power of Makarenko's system and which shows it in all its ruthless indifference to those who failed to accept willingly its doctrines.)

At the time of the original crisis, Makarenko sent for Chobot and said to him:

"You'll have to quit!"

"Where'll I go?"

"I advise you to go where you can knife other people. Just because your comrade wouldn't give up his place to you in the dining room, you jabbed a knife in him, today. Very well, then, find yourself a place where differences are settled with knives (I, 121).

Chobot left, with a final statement from Makarenko that he could return in two weeks time if he found the outside world too difficult.

A month later he returned, gaunt and pale faced.

"I've come back, like you said."

"You didn't find a place to suit you?"

He smiled.

"Didn't I? There are such places. I'll stay in the colony, and I won't use a knife" (I, 122).

Chobot's return marked, as early as the second year of the colony, two important phases in the development of Makarenko's system. On the one hand, the final crisis was passed. Makarenko had won the issue of expulsion and Chobot had returned to vindicate Makarenko's triumph. From that time forward, expulsion was to become a terrifying process which Makarenko resorted to occasionally in order to restore cohesion. The group was never allowed to rest secure: the threat of being pitched to an outside unfriendly world was ever in the background. Makarenko thought, of course, that in expelling Chobot he had secured a further victory in the fight of solidarity, but he did so at a cost, a cost which is dear in any social system and which ought to be pondered over carefully before being paid. Chobot represented a challenge to the system, and Makarenko responded with an extreme form of attack. There was no analysis of Chobot, nor was there any attempt to deal with the knife episode as a symptom of Chobot's own troubles. Chobot was symbolized as a threat to the internal order and was immediately removed from the internal order; in effect, his security was cut ruthlessly

from under him: he was made an example. The group, composed of characters neither better nor worse that Chobot,
had drawn away from him. The destruction of a person's
perceptions of the world, which constitute the essence of a
personal system of values, and thus one's security, is a terrifying weapon to use for the achievement of group solidarity.

This was the other important phase of the episode. From
this moment forward Makarenko had sown the seeds of the
failure of his own system. Chobot, a broken figure, moved
pathetically through the life of the colony until eventually
he failed to see any meaning in his own life and, on May 3,
1925, hanged himself from a rafter in the stable. Of the
events leading up to this more will be said later, but at this
stage it is important to see that Makarenko refused adamantly
to admit of any individuality being more important than
the group. It had to be the group first, and individuality was
to be a reflection of facets of group life that were allowed to
be temporarily displayed through various members of the
group. Such individual action as knifing people must be
prevented in any society, it is true, but the same general
principle—being against individual action—Makarenko applied in all circumstances.

At this time Makarenko moved toward the consolidation
of the group spirit by directing their energies toward tasks
that lay outside the institution. In his conflicting attitudes
toward the fish of Taranets and his own faking of food orders
Makarenko had already shown a tendency to set up the life
of the colony apart from the rest of Soviet society. The boys
had come to regard extant society as a rather corrupted business that had within it little hope of achieving the socialist
millennium. They began to believe that the future, under
Makarenko's guidance, was in their own hands. Gradually
then—and this was to create yet another unsolved problem
—they came to believe that morality resided in the collective
actions of the group, and that what they did collectively was
by definition good.

Makarenko, for his part, encouraged such attitudes, even though he continued to manipulate the scenes in such a way as to put words into the boys' mouths and to arrange actions so as to make them appear to be the results of group decision. Thus, ignoring the realities of life as they then existed, Makarenko directed the boys' energies into a hostility toward the local peasants who, not unnaturally, were not too keen on letting the process of the social ownership of land go too far. At that time, the peasants were in the habit of keeping back part of their crop to make vodka in illicit stills. Discovering some of his boys drunk, Makarenko sought the source; finding it in the farms, he then decided to get the boys to organize themselves into raiding parties and destroy the stills. In this way he would achieve two purposes. The source of the vodka would be destroyed, and, by making the boys go through the actions of destroying it, he would effect, so he hoped, a change in their behavior toward it.

There was no doubt that his proposal was idealistic, to say the least; nor was it designed to help the boys gain an understanding of how the outside world worked. Coming from their own small worlds of depravity and crime, they had little knowledge of the lives of normal people. And for them to find that all normal people in countless daily actions failed to live up to the law, or even deliberately disregarded it, was itself to prove a heady thought, far more intoxicating than the vodka.

The raids, as far as the colony was concerned, were eminently successful. The fact that they secured the enmity of the whole district troubled Makarenko not one whit. What mattered was that the group had found its first task outside the colony. Thus was born the ideal, normative society which Makarenko constantly urged his boys to achieve by contrasting it with the outside real world. Needless to add, the colony gradually identified itself with this ideal society, an identification that was to fail to take heed of many realities and was to raise problems which Makarenko puzzled over almost to

the day he died; these problems constantly presented difficulties in the life of the colony which Makarenko was never
able to put into perspective nor to fully understand.

Within the first two or three years, Makarenko had extracted a set of principles from the group. He had, in a sense,
begun to find meaning in his colony. The production of a
strong in-group, held together by projecting its actions against
an outside world that threatened the attainment of the ideal
world, a group suppressing individuality and finding the
source of all values in its own collective action—this was his
method. What it lacked still was a definitive form through
which it could operate. Makarenko knew that there had to
be an ideal form for the true collective group, and he moved,
in the next phase, to make the ideal form real. He never
doubted that the group—or as he called it, in line with
Marxist orthodoxy, the "collective"—was the social reality.
His next task was to give it definite form. Only when that
was attained could the true task of education proceed—
achieving an isomorphism between the individual and the
collective.

DEVELOPING A GROUP FORM

The attainment of a form came about rather simply, although there is no doubt that deeper influences had been
at work in Makarenko's mind for quite some time. Two years
after the colony had been established, Makarenko, as he
earlier intended to do, had wrung a theory out of the everyday practice. Thus he wrote, as his theoretical analysis of the
question of discipline,

I had ventured to question the correctness of the generally accepted theory of those days, that punishment of any sort is de-
grading, that it s essential to give the fullest possible scope to the
sacred creative impulses of the child, and that the great thing is
to rely solely upon self-organization and self-discipline. I had
also ventured to advance the theory, to me incontrovertible, that,

so long as the collective, and the organs of the collective, had not been created, so long as no traditions existed, and no elementary labour and cultural habits had been formed, the teacher was entitled—nay, was bound!—to use compulsion. I also maintained that it was impossible to base the whole of education on the child's interests, that the cultivation of the sense of duty frequently runs counter to them, especially as these present themselves to the child itself. I called for the education of a strong, toughened individual, capable of performing work that may be both unpleasant and tedious, should the interests of the collective require it.

Summing up, I insisted upon the necessity of the creation of a strong, enthusiastic—if necessary an austere—collective, and of placing all hopes in the collective alone. My opponents could only fling their pedological axioms in my face, starting over and over again from the words "the child" (I, 239–40).

Makarenko presented the above words in a lecture on discipline in 1922; by 1938 he had fully developed his ideas, delivering them to the Narkomprosov of the RSFSR in a series of lectures upon the theme "Problems of Soviet Education in Schools." The second lecture in the series, "Discipline, Regime, Punishment and Encouragement," developed the ideas fully.[1] As early as 1922, then, Makarenko had proceeded to put his ideas into effect. It is also certain that his "barracks-room" discipline was beginning to make his name odorous among higher educational circles. Indeed, as Makarenko proceeded to give the form of his collective a military flavor, criticism of him gradually mounted until it reached the point where he left the Gorki Colony in 1927, having been invited to carry on his work in another colony, set up by the Soviet Police (see Chapter 8), where he would be safe from interference, if not from criticism.[2]

Makarenko never explained satisfactorily how the colony came to have a military aspect. There is, at least, the justifiable reason that these boys, in a war-torn land, had reached the stage where they could reasonably be expected to undergo national military service. Russia was still by no means internationally secure, and some form of military training would not be unnatural for boys of that age. But before long Makarenko changed the whole colony, which had now come to include girls as well, to a completely military basis. Part of the answer rests upon the fact that an army has an extremely idealistic basis, and in all countries over the centuries certain military forms and ideals have sprung up and have remained independent of the individual circumstances. Thus it was that in this, rather than in the extant society which had so thoroughly disillusioned him, Makarenko found a model for the colony's behavior. He cleverly utilized the attractions that military ideals have for adolescents, understanding the fact that the army is always a group that is expending its energies on tasks outside itself.

Very quietly Makarenko mentions the fact that he introduced gymnastics and military drill into the colony, recording, "I do not know myself, how it was that I took up military training with such ardour—it must have been in obedience to some unconscious pedagogical instinct" (I, 342). Before long the colony was incorporated as a unit of the national defense system, the General Military Training Department, and it was issued real rifles. The collective spirit, fostered by raids on vodka stills, was nourished even more strongly as the boys spent their time in military exercises, becoming so proficient that

By the winter our skirmishing lines were executing extremely interesting and complicated movements all over the territory of our group of farmsteads. With grace and methodical accuracy we carried out assaults on given targets—huts and storerooms—assaults crowned by bayonet attacks and by the panic which seized the impressionable souls of their proprietors and proprietresses.

. . . .

During training I was exacting and inexorable, like a true commander; and the boys thoroughly approved of this. Thus were the foundations of a new game laid, that game which subsequently became one of the main themes of our life (I, 342–43).

A military cast in the life of the colony, then, was received happily. The idea of the army, being the one universal institution in which the group always comes first explicitly and without any thought of challenge, fostered collectivity. The boys took quite naturally to it; and for Makarenko there is no doubt that he enjoyed playing the role of military commander.

The development of the colony into a quasi-military academy proceeded rapidly. Makarenko makes clever use of the passive voice in recording that

It was just at this time that the rule was introduced into the colony: to reply to every order, in token of confirmation and consent, with the words "very good!", accompanying this splendid reply with the flourish of the Pioneer salute. It was at this time, too, that bugles were introduced to the colony.

Hitherto our signals had been given by means of the bell left over from the former colony. Now we bought two bugles, and some of the boys went daily to the town to take lessons from the bandmaster in playing the bugle from notes. Signals for all occasions occurring in colony life were committed to paper, and by the winter we were able to dispense with the bell. The bugler went on to my porch of a morning, now, and flung over the colony the melodious, sonorous sounds of the signal (I, 344).

There is no doubt that the sound of the bugles was music for Makarenko's soul. As all of this external formalization occurred, two significant internal forms were established, both of which were somewhat inimical to the prevailing educational and social thought but which later were to be justified. On the one hand the element of competition was introduced, and on the other the colony divided up into "detachments."

The development of these two forms occurred at the same time, each helping to occasion the other. Throughout the years that these developments were occurring, the members of the colony were working at a considerable number of tasks. The day had been divided into two halves: there was productive work, chiefly farming and agricultural shop work, and then school, where lessons proceeded according to the traditional methods although the content had been given a new twist. Makarenko always concerned himself with the tasks outside the school, leaving the jobs of formal instruction to the teachers, a rather significant feature. Indeed, as the colony progressed, Makarenko never bothered himself very much with the formal aspects of education and in fact never really grappled with the problems of learning theory or of epistemology.

It was the need to increase productivity on the one hand and on the other to get the children to perform unpleasant but necessary tasks that brought out the competitive element. In the winter of 1923 loads of firewood had to be brought in from the forest, and in order to lighten their task the boys began to organize themselves into groups and to compete in bringing in the greatest number of loads. This was readily sanctioned by Makarenko, who saw its relation to the military ideal. The word "detachment," which was criticized by the child-centered theorists, who were in turn derided by Makarenko as "pedagogical scribblers," was derived from the organization of the Russian guerilla irregulars, and thus it was a word that carried romantic overtones. The use of the word by the boys "revived the familiar, beloved image of that other detachment, of which, if there were no actual memories, there were innumerable tales and legends" (I, 371). In defense of the use of detachments, Makarenko argued that

> I had no wish to interfere with the half-conscious play of the revolutionary instincts of our colonists. The pedagogical scriveners who criticized so harshly our detachments and our military games were simply incapable of understanding what it all was about. The word detachment held no pleasing associations for those whom detachments had once given short shrift—seizing their apartments and ignoring their psychology, shooting right and left from their three-inch guns, without respect for their science or their thought-wrinkled brows.

But there was no help for it. Ignoring the tastes of our critics, the colony began with a detachment (I, 371).

The organization into detachments went ahead in two directions. On the one hand there were the permanent detachments, to which each person belonged, presided over by a chosen boy, called a commander; and there were the temporary detachments, called mixed detachments, which were called into being for the achievement of specific tasks and headed by a temporary commander. The mixed detachments, as the name implies, were made up of members from all the permanent detachments. In addition to this there developed a governing body called the commanders' council, with Makarenko as the ex-officio chairman. Makarenko, in line with his developing ideas of a system that was external to the members, saw no particular virtue in the election of the commanders. Gradually election came to be used, but Makarenko never agreed with it. He expressed himself quite strongly on this point: "... I myself never considered, and still do not consider, such free election as an achievement" (I, 374). In addition to the appointment of commanders, Makarenko saw that they had absolute authority, which in his opinion was a good thing. Thus he wrote,

The absolute authority of our commanders during work, and their responsibility from the very first, seemed to us a most important point, and Sherre [one of the commanders] was the first to insist that one of the members of the colony should be responsible for discipline, for the implements, for the work itself, and for its quality. Not a single rational person would now be found to raise objections to these demands, and even then, I think, it was only the pundits who had any objections (I, 375–76).

There was an attempt to share authority by giving each person in the colony, so far as was possible, a turn at being a commander of one of the mixed, temporary detachments. Nevertheless, the whole system of the detachment organization had a primary end in view, the final perfection of the form of collective life, and it achieved, therefore, the important job of creating recognized lines of authority. Makarenko wrote that "This [system of commanders] created an extremely intricate chain of subordination in the colony, in which it was impossible for individual members to become unduly conspicuous, or to predominate in the collective" (I, 379).

By the end of 1923 the collective system had been fairly well established. The idealization of the collective and the suppression of individuality had been achieved, although it was as yet unrefined. Nevertheless, Makarenko had developed certain cardinal principles. At times the colony was encouraged to be merciless with individuals, as is illustrated by the case of the bricklayer and chimney-builder, Artemi. Artemi came from the town to build a stove and was, apparently, an inexperienced artisan who was nevertheless boastful. The boys, in their own inimitable manner, urged him on to tell tales of his skill to which Artemi obligingly responded. Later the chimney collapsed, and Makarenko was ready to point out that "his name remained for long a synonym for a know-nothing braggart and a bungler" (I, 357).

THE ACHIEVEMENT OF THE COLLECTIVE

In the original settlement at Poltava, Makarenko had developed the beginnings of his system. The notion of the priority of the group had been established, and Makarenko had been successful in forging a strongly-knit solidarity that had been successful in preventing the colony from disintegrating as it had early threatened to. Despite this, the system had a long way to go before it could be called sophisticated, and Makarenko turned his attention next to the refinement of the system. Many problems remained unsolved, and to the time of his death many were to remain so. But, as 1923 drew to a close, Makarenko had made certain significant gains in the creation of the new Soviet man.

In 1923 he had been successful in having a nearby deserted noble estate given to him as a more promising site for his colony, and during that year repairs had been effected that enabled him to move the colonists across just before the onset of winter. The move was symbolic. As Makarenko developed the notion of finding targets of action outside the colony, so he also realized that in keeping his system moving forward it had to have an element of change, of novelty. For him, a change to a new location meant a psychological change both for himself and for his charges. It meant that they would all begin under fresh circumstances that much further along the line of social development. In addition, it meant that the past would cease to exist in any real sense and would become idealistically reconstructed in the minds of the children. In a new location only the rosy outlines of former years would be retained.

For Makarenko the removal of the past was a serious element of his thinking. He recorded that "as far back as 1922 I had asked the Commission [for Juvenile Delinquency] not to send me any more personal records" (I, 405). That was because he considered that "the principal method for the re-education of delinquents [pravonarushitelei [3]] should be based on a complete ignoring of the past, especially past crimes" (I, 404). It was necessary to do this because otherwise the problems of re-education would be hampered by the memories of past experiences.

The job was to "re-educate him [the besprizornik] on new lines, that is to say, in such a manner that he should become not merely a harmless member of society but also an active worker in the new epoch" (I, 403). The next stage in this re-education, then, was begun with the transfer. By October 1923 the colony numbered eighty.

In appearance, all its members with few exceptions were equally spruce, and all flaunted a military bearing. We already had splendid marching columns, their vanguard adorned by four buglers and eight drummers. We had a banner too, a lovely silk one, and embroidered in silk—a present from the Ukrainian People's Commissariat for Education, on the occasion of our third anniversary.

. . . .

On the 3rd of October, 1923, such a column streamed across the colony drill ground.

. . . .

At twelve noon, a representative of the Gubernia Department of Public Education signed the deed for the handing over of the estate of the Gorky Colony, and stood aside. I gave the order: "To the colours—attention!" (I, 435–37).

Then the removal began which is best told in Makarenko's own words. As he tells it, it is eminently clear that the first victory was his, and a new era had indeed begun. Having given his order,

The boys drew themselves up for the salute, the drums thundered, the bugles sounded for the march past of the colours. The flag brigade brought the banner out of the office. Bearing it on our right flank, we bade no farewell to the old place, though we harboured not the slightest hostility to it. We just didn't like looking back. Nor did we glance back when the columns of our colony, shattering the silence of the fields with its drum beats, . . . descended to the grassy valley of the Kolomak, marching towards the new bridge built by the members of our colony.

The whole staff and a number of villagers from Goncharovka were gathered in the yard at Trepke, and the columns of the new colony members, in all their glory, stood to attention in honour of the Gorky banner. We had entered upon a new era (I, 437–38).

CHAPTER 7

THE MYSTIQUE OF THE COLLECTIVE

NEW DIRECTIONS IN MAKARENKO'S THOUGHT

Life at the old estate at Poltava had been pre-eminently concerned with an attempt to find some meaning in the defiant
normlessness of the besprizorniki—an attempt to get them to
act together according to some rational, predictable manner.
Makarenko had been cured early of his overidealistic simplification of the problem, and he realized that he was far from
the truth in supposing that the besprizorniki would only
have to be exposed to a better life for their adoption of it to
be automatic. On the contrary, the besprizorniki had to be
led, figuratively, by the scruffs of their necks.

What Makarenko did was to work empirically, to test out
solutions, withdrawing where he felt too much resistance,
pressing ahead when he found an opening. All along he relied on what seems to be a form of intuition, an intuition that
guides a person in the delicate problem of handling human
relations. Once Makarenko had achieved any sort of pattern,
he quickly hardened it into an established practice. Within
a few years he had achieved remarkable success in handling
group relations and in directing and controlling human behavior. The difficulty that he felt, by 1923, was a lack of understanding on his own part of the processes underlying his

successful empirically-derived techniques. Makarenko was plainly not satisfied with his ability to control group behavior only within certain limits. The job of creating the new Soviet man had to be more thorough than that and he saw two distinct problems ahead of himself. He knew nothing about the processes of individual action and its relationships to the group; neither did he know anything about the actual group processes through which he was able to secure his results.

The period from October, 1923, to March, 1926—approximately two and one-half years—marks a significant change in the directions of his thought. In these years, covered by the second volume of *The Road to Life,* Makarenko became engrossed in the problems of what underlay group processes. These problems came up in his mind in a great variety of ways, and a glance at some of them will reveal both their complexity and the difficulties that he must have had in attempting their solution. Thus, he became concerned with the nature of the imperative behind the collective, the location of authority in the collective, the relation of the individual to the collective, the nature of the "adhesive" that binds a collective together, and even with the meaning and value of his own life. These problems are no mean ones for any educator to work with. During this period Makarenko came under a considerable amount of critical investigation, chiefly at the regional level, and he felt impelled to justify his methods, apart from any personal desires to justify his own life.

At the same time, however, Makarenko never seriously doubted the fundamental value of the collective, at least insofar as his own testimony reveals the true nature of his thought, and he never wavered from his original idealistic vision of the Soviet utopia. The whole direction of his thought, then, is toward the discovery of the hidden realities that govern the operation of group life. Although, apart from a few fleeting references, he never seemed to recognize it, he was seeking to find the spirit of the group, its mystique.

THE IMPERATIVE BEHIND THE COLLECTIVE

In saying that Makarenko never doubted the fundamental value of the collective it is implied that he always accepted it as the starting point of social organization and as the basic unit on which all human activities hinge. In making this assumption he was in line with orthodox Marxist views and, to a large extent, with a considerable body of opinion in the West. Social theorists like Sumner,[1] for example, hold with the primacy of the group. In making this assumption, which is often the result of a naïve, direct, empirical observation, there are two issues that can be raised, and the solution given to them will directly influence the type of social theory that is constructed upon them. On the one hand, the group can be considered as, hypothetically, nothing more than the technical instrument of effective action. That is, it can be seen to be simply a useful tool for the accomplishment of human purposes, without there being any attempt to discover the fundamental nature of those purposes. On the other hand, the group may be thought of as an absolute entity in and of itself, that is, an organic view which sees the individual as an element of the greater unity.

For Makarenko this problem was never posed in exactly this form, and this seems partly due to his failure to analyze his problems philosophically. This was due, no doubt, to his own lack of philosophical knowledge and was reinforced by his own conceit in his successful ability as a practical man. Thus, in the second volume of *The Road to Life,* when Makarenko searched for the truth behind the collective, he did so from the implicit, unexamined assumption that the social group is absolute. The problem, as he saw it, was to find the true nature of the social group's authority over the individual, but with the express purpose of being able to control the exercising of that authority to the better achievement of social purposes. The problem became somewhat biased from its beginnings in that Makarenko never wanted to come up with a solution that released the individual from the collective grip. Rather, he felt from the beginning that the group was primary and he sought to find the ultimate basis on which his authority rested.

This sort of problem became significant for him because it arose in the context of daily life. When the *structure* of the socialist ideal had been achieved, it should follow, quite naturally, that human life would act out its desired course. The desired course was that of working together harmoniously for the achieving of the socialist ideal. Thus, in Poltava, when the form had been achieved and had been successfully and symbolically transferred to Trepke, it should have followed as night the day that the children would begin to work together in one harmonious unit. Sadly enough such a naïve faith in the power of the environment was not supported by the evidence. Because of his implicit faith in the primacy of the collective and because he was still confused about the true nature of collective action, Makarenko redoubled his efforts in the direction of finding what further factors prevented the children from acting completely in accord with the socialist ideal. Problems of the failure or the difficulty of running a collective never stemmed, in his view, from the possibility that the individual might at times be in opposition to the group, that there could be a realm of individual life, but rather that he had not yet fully understood the true nature of the collective and mastered its control. Thus he looked at failure on the part of the children as his failure to discover hidden factors.

These hidden factors were sought by Makarenko in his usual manner. He continued to make observations about his colonists, to manipulate the environment, and to verbalize his findings in a dialectic form through which he hoped to work toward the truth. One of the targets of his attention was the question of motivation. The two extreme methods of getting human action to follow the proper structure of society were raised in a discussion between Olya, one of the girls in the colony, and several of its boys. The boys, for their part, represented the forces of coercion and compulsion while Olya represented reason. The conversation concerned work in the commune, and Olya remarked that

"The peasants ought to work still better in a commune."

"What makes you think so?" asked Pavel Pavlovitch gently.
. . . .

"They ought to!" said Olya. "You know what 'ought to' means, don't you? Its as plain as two and two is four." ...

Karabanov ... could not refrain from taking part in the verbal gymnastics.

"Olya's right," he said. " 'Ought to' means they must be taken in hand and compelled. . . ."

"And how are you going to compel them?" asked Pavel Pavlovitch.

"Somehow or other," said Semyon, warming up to the subject. "How does one compel people? By force! Just you hand all your muzhiks to me and in a week they'll be working like lambs, and in two weeks they'll be thanking me."

Pavel Pavlovitch screwed up his eyes.

"And what's your force? A sock in the jaw?"

Semyon flopped down on the bench laughing, and Burun explained, restrained contempt in his voice:

"Sock in the jaw— Nuts! The real force is a revolver."

Olya turned her face slowly towards him, instructing him patiently:

"It's *you* who don't understand. If people *ought* to do a thing, they'll do it without a revolver. They'll do it of their own free will. You only have to tell them properly, explain." *

In this conversation, of which a considerable amount more is recorded, Makarenko gave the fundamental proposition

* Makarenko, A. S., *The Road to Life*, Foreign Languages Publishing House, Moscow, 1955, vol. II, pp. 31–33. Quotations in this chapter all come from this edition, and the volume number and pages are given in parentheses at the end of the quoted material.

of the volume. He stated his concern with finding the basis of the *oughtness* underlying the group life.

Life in the Trepke estate followed much the same pattern as it did the previous years. The children worked in the fields, in the shops, and in the school house. The goals of life were to make the colony self-supporting in food and at the same time to produce goods which could be sold outside the colony in order to buy those things which had to come in from the towns. Life at Trepke was organized, however, according to the detachment system, and it was highly routinized with its military atmosphere. It was in this sort of framework that Makarenko became concerned with the fundamental problem of compulsion and acceptance.

When it came to examining the problem of compulsion, Makarenko very soon saw that it was largely a question of motivation, and he attempted to examine more deeply the sources of motivation. He always had a belief in the power of reason—although he didn't recognize this so very explicitly —but he did gradually come to see that reason in the form of a rational explanation was not sufficient. In moving toward an understanding of the oughtness of behavior, Makarenko was concerned, not with whether the collective has any real demands upon the individual, but with the manner of making the demands of the collective so apparent and appealing that it would consequentially influence behavior in the direction of accepting the group norms.

THE INDIVIDUAL AND THE COLLECTIVE

This sort of framework of thinking soon required Makarenko to look at the instances of individual behavior, and the second volume is largely a record of individual actions. This was a favorite method of Makarenko's, and in large measure the individual problems that he examined at Trepke were those of Chobot. This person, it will be remembered from the previous chapter, tested the limits of the system.

As Chobot's tragic death testified, the system was never large enough to hold him. For Makarenko, this problem was not recognized. He had always accepted a certain amount of "waste," and Chobot's suicide was not, in Makarenko's view, an indictment of the system or of the collective itself. Rather, Makarenko thought that the suicide was due in large measure to his present inability to control all aspects of the educational process, and his inability to inculcate in all the colonists a desire to become fully identified with the group. Thus Chobot became an educational failure, and it is singularly astonishing to see the calm and relief with which his death was accepted. Indeed, Chobot's death did not make Makarenko examine the system at all in its fundamental propositions but instead set him thinking about the educational failure of making Chobot conform to the collective life.

Very early in the book, in the conversation between Olya and the boys, mentioned above, the problem became restated as: "What's the good of explaining, if a chap *wants* to be a kulak?" (II, 33). Chobot was always identified as one who wanted to be a kulak, a kulak—being the symbol of the individual person who resisted complete absorption into the collective life—having more than the simple connotation of the small farmer.

The Gorki Colony had taken a number of girls into its ranks a few years before, and at the time of the move to Trepke the problem of romance was raised. Makarenko stated quite plainly that he opposed the notions of romantic love for the very simple reason that loyalties became divided —the individual became torn between serving the wider demands of collective life on the one hand and the narrower demands of the individual person on the other. For Makarenko, love created groups that, by their very nature, set themselves apart from the wider society. When it became apparent to everyone that Chobot was in love, Makarenko seized the opportunity to work out the issue with real people.

The beginning of the episode for Chobot, as Makarenko saw him, was hardly propitious:

> The plight of Chobot was still sadder. He was a gloomy passionate individual, without a single distinctive trait. He had signalized his entry into the colony by a conflict involving the use of knives, but had since then steadily submitted to discipline, although always holding aloof from the seething centres of our life.
> . . . .
> The whole colony knew that Chobot was passionately in love with Natasha Petrenko.
> . . . .
> I could not believe that this child was capable of loving Chobot, but the boys contradicted me in unison:
> "Who? Natasha? Why, she'd go through fire and water for Chobot without a moment's hesitation!" (II, 117–19).

The case took its first serious turn when Chobot rose to the defense of Natasha. She was the ward of Moussi Karpovitch, a farmer on a small property near the colony, and was considerably ill-used by Moussi. One day Moussi took to whipping her with a pair of horse reins when she failed to dry some of the washing, and Chobot, catching Moussi in the act, attacked him. The farmer was no match for the vigorous youth, who soon reduced Moussi to a terrified, quivering heap in the corner. Moussi's cries for help attracted some of the other boys who dragged Chobot off before the fury had run its complete course. The upshot was for Natasha to be made a member of the colony.

For the next year or so, the question of Chobot and Natasha remained relatively dormant. Already, however, the threat had been posed, and throughout that time there was a tension in the colony, doubtless of Makarenko's own making, about the division of loyalties that such romance could bring. During that period, the consolidation of the colony into an even firmer collective took place, and the solidarity of the collective was thrown into greater relief by the contrast that Chobot afforded. The boys, who for their part had been quite sympathetic with Chobot, became, under Makarenko's influence, gradually estranged. And in the process of making this consolidation, Makarenko continued to use an old device that he found to work: an appeal to solidarity by posing an outside threat, in this case the weakening of the collective by the love of Chobot and Natasha. The girl, curiously enough, never came in for any criticism, and Chobot alone had to bear the responsibility for the creation and maintenance of the affair.

In describing the growth of the collective, Makarenko made effective use of Chobot, yet he kept the two issues completely separated, and it seems curious, to say the least, that he failed to see that the whole success he enjoyed in consolidating his system was due completely to the chance Chobot afforded him of pointing out to the other boys the threat that existed to group life. Makarenko attempted to win Chobot back into the fold, and had he been successful it is interesting to speculate on what issue or person he would have seized to keep the threat alive.

Every chance he could, Makarenko saw threats from the outside, and another extremely curious action was his finding threats from the representatives of the government. Thus he used the person of Maria Kondratyevna Bokova as an exemplar for his charges. Maria Kondratyevna was an official of the Social Education Department who came to inspect the colony periodically. She was a young attractive person, given to fashionable clothing, and Makarenko was quick to see the possibility of furthering his own purposes. He represented Maria as a threat from external authority and, when she demurred upon being asked to join in the work of the colony on her visits, his point was made. The colonists of course scored a considerable victory when eventually Maria Kondratyevna did one day join in their work, and Makarenko recorded his triumph at the end of the day's harvesting when the whole group engaged in relaxations:

It was gay and noisy at the tables in the garden, and Maria Kondratyevna was ready to weep for all sorts of reasons—because she was tired, because she loved the colonists, because in her, too, the true law of humanity had been revived, because she, too, had tasted the delights of a free, working collective.

"Well, was your work too easy?" Burun asked her.

"I don't know," said Maria Kondratyevna. "It was hard, I suppose, but that's not the point. Such work is happiness, anyhow" (II, 174–75).

Makarenko never failed to make use of the threat of expulsion to achieve this solidarity, and when Oprishko, one of the boys, was accused of continued drunkenness, the problem was not in the drunkenness, nor in any possible causes of it within the colony. The problem was simply a violation of rules, and Makarenko's treatment was quite summary; he simply ordered the immediate expulsion of the offender.

As 1925 neared an end, Makarenko felt that the colony had achieved, with one blemish, a high state of perfection. The blemish was Chobot, and Makarenko recorded quite simply that "Chobot was an obstacle to our progress, and I could not manage him" (II, 258).

The crisis with Chobot was near. Chobot had always had an independent spirit, it will be remembered, and he had been severely treated very early in the days of the colony by his temporary expulsion for fighting with a knife. Natasha, from the time she entered the colony, rapidly became amenable to the discipline and life and before long she too was absorbed in the spirit of working toward goals. Being somewhat studious, Natasha was susceptible to the attractions of the school at the Rabfak to which the youths went after they left the colony if they wanted to pursue their education. Chobot, however, was for a quiet life as a village farmer, married to Natasha. When Chobot submitted his proposal to her, she went to Makarenko and asked him for an answer to give Chobot. It will be argued, of course, that in going to Makarenko she already knew what answer she wanted, but it was a symptom of the colonists that in moments of decision they proved themselves incapable of acting alone, and not infrequently did they go to Makarenko for an answer.

Chobot was, not surprisingly, refused. Makarenko counseled Natasha to continue with her studies, reminding her of the wider duties she owed to Soviet society. When Chobot had to be informed, even Makarenko hesitated, fidgeting with the keys and drawers of his desk. Chobot didn't have to be told, but, guessing the truth, left the room. The description of the incident is frightening.

> "Chobot!" I shouted.
> He did not seem to hear me, but straightened himself and went away without looking back at me, silent and light-footed as a ghost (II, 262).

After a period of despondency, Chobot passed a rope over a rafter in the stables, placed the noose around his neck, and jumped. Makarenko simply recorded that "Chobot hanged himself on the evening of May the 3rd" (II, 269).

The reactions of the colonists were astonishing. None, according to Makarenko, displayed any grief. One colonist, Lapot, was condemning in his observations: "He lived and died a kulak, and it was greed which killed him" (II, 270). Another colonist, Koval, refused to attend the funeral, saying, "I would hang fellows like Chobot myself—getting under people's feet with their idiotic affairs" (II, 270). These are extremely uncharitable comments to come from adolescents, unfortunate as they may have been, and it raises disturbing questions about the system under which they had formed their values. For the whole colony the death of Chobot had great significance. More than anything, the colony was relieved at getting rid of what was becoming an embarrassment for them, and Makarenko found in Chobot's death, not a cause for reflection but a new principle to direct the colony. Thus, in musing over Chobot, Makarenko's thoughts took the following turn:

> On the way back I pondered over the paths open to our colony. A full-grown crisis seemed to have sprung up in our midst, and many of the things I valued most were threatening to hurl

themselves into an abyss—things bright and living, created almost miraculously during five years of work by the collective, things the immense value of which no conventional modesty could make me conceal from myself.

In a collective like ours the obscurity of individual paths could not form a crisis. Individual paths are never clearly defined. And what could a clearly defined individual path imply? Nothing but isolation from the collective, concentrated pettiness—the old tedious thought of where bread for the morrow was to come from, of the eternally vaunted qualifications. And what qualifications? Carpenter, cobbler, miller. . . . No, no, I am perfectly convinced that for a sixteen-year-old boy in our Soviet life the most precious qualification is the qualification of the fighter and the human being.

I thought of the strength of the colonists' collective, and suddenly I realized what was wrong. Why, of course—how could I have taken so long to discover it? It had come about because we were at a standstill. A standstill can never be allowed in the life of a collective (II, 272–73).

Thus emerged the principle of continued growth and change in the life of the colony. What Makarenko did was to make explicit to himself, for the first time, the principle of constantly directing the energies of the colony toward goals which lay outside the collective itself. Thus, solidarity became the reaction to a challenge. As an educational problem, the task of education was, according to Makarenko's early theory, one of finding a set of situations that menace the individual and which urge him into a collective response. Once the collective response has been made, then the educational process is essentially one of continuing the challenges in such a way that responses need to be continually made.

To justify such a theory, of course, there have to be some good reasons. On the one hand the obvious suggestion is an implicit Hegelianism which Makarenko never fully realized. Certainly in none of his works does he betray any knowledge of the movement of German Idealism. For the present analysis there are two more immediate issues that need to be considered: the source of the challenges and the direction in which the progression of experiences proceeds. At the time that his theory was evolved, the challenges came from Makarenko's own interpretation of the needs of the group rather than from the group itself. Makarenko became the source of a supposedly beneficent utilitarianism. The progression of experiences was again a matter of Makarenko's own judgment, and he alone was the judge of the adequacy of the outcomes. Thus the colonists learned their values from Makarenko's own approval and disapproval of their actions. The problem that remained even after these two issues were settled was that of the source from which Makarenko got his authority.

THE ULTIMATE SOURCES OF EDUCATIONAL
AUTHORITY

What was happening to these young people under Makarenko's care was that, in essence, they were undergoing a program of deliberate moral conditioning. The fact that the source of the morality was at times obscure nevertheless does not alter the situation. Makarenko himself, it seems certain, was confused and insecure in his possession of authority. The confusion doubtless arose from the peculiar situation in which any form of order was preferable to the social chaos of the early twenties; but as the decade progressed, and as the world gradually assumed a clearer and more definite order, then the need for a clarification of the source of authority became necessary. If indeed the besprizorniki were being educated, then they obviously had to be educated in accord with the moral dictates of the society into which they were ultimately to enter. Education had to fit them to take a place within some social order, even if they were to change it.

During this period Makarenko clearly did not know what the moral order was, nor did he have any clear idea of the nature of the society into which these adolescents would move. Working as he did with marginal people in an almost closed society, he set up norms and expectations that, in the first instance, enabled him to get a rational, workable basis for the colony. Then, as the life proceeded, he sought to find a means whereby he could implement desired behavior changes so that the educational ideal he set up would be attained. That much is clear. He instituted a set of challenging situations to keep the group moving forward, and he himself provided the criteria of evaluation. The only difficulty with the system was that Makarenko was working for the attainment of an ideal which he had himself drawn from the revolutionary movement. There were few real daily-life problems of the outside world seeping through into the colony because it was in effect isolated as well as self-contained. Thus, his colony was not as useful as he thought it would be in teaching children to live in the outside world.

Because the ultimate source of authority for his actions came from his own perceptions of what was necessary to produce people who would build a better social world, Makarenko was working in conflict with the outside social order. As previously related incidents have shown, Makarenko actually set his colonists up in opposition to the outside world. This awkward situation brought with it considerable difficulties for him during this period, and Makarenko was troubled by the obvious discrepancy between his own educational goals and processes on the one hand and those of the outside society on the other. For one very obvious reason, once the colonists had been brought under firm social control, the continued seeking of the challenges in the outside society would lead to a growing estrangement between his colony and extant Soviet society. In effect, his charges would become progressively unfit to enter Soviet society because of the discrepancy between their values and those that would surround them.

This conflict marks a distinct stage in the evolution of Makarenko's thought, and it raised problems that preoccupied him until his last days, problems of which he was never certain in his solutions. There were two obvious sources of the problems. On the one hand his methods were in direct contrast with the officially endorsed policy of Soviet education during the twenties. The general policy was, as the next section will show, concerned with realizing the values of the individual personality, and with a decidedly democratic, child-centered rationale for the whole educative process. On the other hand, Makarenko never shook off the cultural values of Russian life that had come through for generations, and at times he is given to a meditation on ultimate values that reveals a basic insecurity in his belief in the absolute primacy of the group. In the development of his educational theory, the problems from these two sources were to harass him to such an extent that he was unable ever to formulate his theories completely successfully.

CONFLICT WITH OFFICIAL EDUCATIONAL POLICY

Throughout all of Makarenko's writings there is a continued attitude of contempt for the official authorities controlling education, an attitude which at times seems somewhat surprising. When the organization of the colony along military lines, with its extremely intricate patterns of control and subordination, is considered, it seems incompatible that Makarenko should resent authority. He spent a considerable amount of his time exhorting his charges to work for the attainment of the completely solidaristic state and was most ruthless in dealing with those who failed to abide by the rules of the organization. Yet in his own behavior he was constantly at odds with the outside official authorities.

A satisfactory explanation of this behavior is hard to find, and it seems most likely that Makarenko was confused and uncertain of the source of his own revolt. It is very likely true that he had developed an idealized form of society in which everything worked so smoothly that he had acquired a trained incapacity to see the usual world, and normal people, in any sort of relation to the ideal. On the other hand, he was himself unsophisticated in higher thought, and much of his antagonism to the authorities came from his failure to understand the methods and ideas which they were implementing. Thus, one of his most frequent jibes at them is with respect to their scientific procedures.

Very early in the days of the Trepke occupation the Kharkov Pedagogical Institute sent two young student-teachers, K. Varskaya and R. Landsberg, on an observational visit to the colony. Makarenko recorded their visits, although his description is crude caricature designed to show up the students in the worst possible light. Makarenko distorted their questions and, by a not so very clever piece of writing, made it appear that he scored a considerable victory. One of the girl student-teachers, K. Varskaya, began the conversation that is recorded.

> "Do you have a pedological room?"
> "We have no pedological room."
> "How do you study personality, then?"
> "The personality of the child?" I asked as gravely as I could.
> "Yes, of course. The personality of your pupil."
> "Why should it be studied?"
> "Why? How can you work otherwise? How can you work on material you know nothing about?"
> . . . .
> "What dominants predominate among your charges?" asked K. Varskaya, sternly resolute.
> "If the personality is not studied in the colony," interpolated R. Landsberg quietly, "it's no use talking about dominants."
> "Not at all," I said seriously. "I can tell you something about dominants. The same dominants predominate here as they do with yourselves" (II, 63–64).

After this sort of introduction, Makarenko proceeded to treat the two young girls as if they were members of his own colony and, chiefly by pointing out their youth and inexperience to them, gently ridiculed them. He did not, for example, produce any counter arguments, but relied instead on the condescension that age often affects toward the young. The two young girl students left the colony subdued and thoughtful, although by no means in possession of Makarenko's arguments against pedology.

The encounters with the outside world were not always so fortunate, and Makarenko became the subject of certain critical investigation which he could not shrug off so condescendingly. Thus when Lyubov Dzhurinskaya, an inspector from the Peoples' Commissariat for Education, came to make an inspection, Makarenko reported that "I received her, as I usually received inspectors, with the caution of a wolf accustomed to being hunted" (II, 238).

Dzhurinskaya's visit was prompted by complaints that had reached the Commissariat about Makarenko's methods, especially his methods of punishment. At the time, punishment in the official child-centered pedagogy was banned, absolutely in spirit if not explicitly in the letter of the law. Makarenko agreed that he did punish by such means as depriving his children of their dinner, but insisted that it was a necessary pedagogical step. To explain his relative ignorance of the prevailing educational theories, Makarenko exclaimed

"... I don't read the writings of all sorts of scribes."
"You don't read works on pedology! D'you mean it?" [she asked]
"I gave up reading them three years ago."
"You ought to be ashamed! Do you read at all?"
"I read a lot. And I'm not ashamed—bear that in mind! And I'm extremely sorry for those who do read books on pedology."
"I shall have to convert you—really, I shall! We've got to have Soviet pedagogics."
I decided to bring the discussion to an end, and said to Lyubov Savelyevna:
"Look here! I'm not going to argue. I'm profoundly convinced that here, in the colony, we have real Soviet pedagogics. More, that ours is communist education. You can be convinced either

by experience, or by serious research—a work on the subject! Such things are not to be decided in mere conversation.
. . . .
"But I shall go on doing things the way I consider necessary, and as best I can" (II, 240–41).

Although Makarenko reported that Dzhurinskaya went away satisfied with his work, the criticisms of his conduct of the colony continued. On the one hand Makarenko was criticized for developing his own methods instead of Soviet ones, and on the other for using discipline and competition which were antipathetic to the current practice. Makarenko was indignant at the accusation that he used his own methods; thus, when an inspector reported that the purpose of his visit was to look into Makarenko's methods, the hurt reply was

"I protest categorically," I said. "There's no such thing as *my* method."
"What method do you use then?"
"The usual Soviet method."
Bregel smiled sourly (II, 275).

In the same inspection, Chaikin, a professor of pedagogics, made certain extremely critical observations which bothered Makarenko for some time to come. The basis of Chaikin's criticisms depended upon the fact that Makarenko used competition among his detachments for the purpose of increasing production. This was before the period of *Stakhanovism* (see below, Chapter 9), and such methods were officially discountenanced. Thus Chaikin summed up his criticisms in the following words:

"we consider competition a method grossly bourgeois, inasmuch as it substitutes for the direct attitude to things, an indirect one. . . . [Y]ou give pocket money to your charges . . . and the amount of the pocket money is not the same for everyone, but varies in accordance, so to say, with each one's deserts" (II, 277).

Makarenko had no answer for Chaikin and, unlike his tactics with the girl students who had visited the colony, he was unable to smother Chaikin with a gush of superiority. Instead, Makarenko decided in his mind that Chaikin was a "bore" and needed "a good whipping, ... with an ordinary belt such as a worker keeps his trousers up with" (II, 277).

To the criticisms of his methods Makarenko had no ready answer. He was unable to articulate the methods that he employed in terms that provided a valid explanation, and in any case he was still unsure of the goals that he was seeking. In fairness to Makarenko, the critics were themselves uncertain of the methods by which Soviet education should be carried forward, and many of the criticisms of Makarenko were negative and carping rather than positive and suggestive. But the criticisms, despite Makarenko's apparently confident rebuttal of them, left their sting, and Makarenko began to work them over in his mind continually.

THE LESSONS OF TREPKE

As the days at Trepke drew to a close, the collective wavered. A large number of the original older boys had reached the age where they had to go on in life, and most of them went on to the Rabfak, a school within the factory system, leaving Makarenko concerned with the excessive juvenility of the colony. In his mind the earlier principle kept reasserting itself: A standstill can't be allowed in the life of the collective. Makarenko made a move toward a change, deciding once more that a change of location would be a helpful stimulus.

The new location that he sought was the Popov estate in which he proposed to care for eight hundred besprizorniki. This abandoned palace was in such bad condition that it needed considerable repairs, the estimates for which, however, when submitted to the People's Commissariat for Finance, were rejected. Thus, in Makarenko's simple words, "The dream died." Meanwhile, the children's colony at Kuryazh, outside Kharkov, was in a beggarly condition.

Upon hearing a description of the four hundred inmates and their condition, Makarenko said that the description seemed to be "a conglomeration of doubtful anecdotes, concocted by a foul-minded pervert, a misanthrope and a cynic" (II, 304).

Despite the filth and despair of the Kuryazh colony, it had its attractions for Makarenko. Not the least among these was the promise by the Department of Public Education that he could work there in peace. Thus, an inspector of the department, Yuryev, made the following offer: "We'll give you carte blanche. Do what you like. Kuryazh is in a ghastly state" (II, 306). The thought of being free again of the irritations of the officials of the department was tempting. In addition, the Kuryazh colony would provide an effective challenge to the colony at Trepke which would be transferred *in toto.* There were many pondered factors involved in the decision, and once again these came to his mind. The chance to test his methods yet further was most appealing.

The years at Trepke had been devoted to a search to understand the group processes and the relation of the individual to the collective. These two issues Makarenko failed to solve to his own satisfaction in those years, although he made considerable progress in ordering them in his mind. He had realized early that the collective was built around a creative minority who were freely followed by the majority, a minority that Makarenko called a "nucleus" (II, 211), and not so long afterwards he established the principle of the need for a constant challenge.

The mystique of the group, the ultimate essence that constituted its unique quality as a group, evaded him, however. This caused him no little trouble, and at times in his thinking he got very close to mysticism. One night, in thinking over the issue, he mused thus:

The world seemed to me a sort of magic potion of the most complex consistency—delicious, seductive. But it was impossible to resolve it into its ingredients, and no one could tell what bitternesses were dissolved in it. At such moments a man is beset by philosophical conjectures, by the longing to grasp the incomprehensible (II, 207–8).

In the same train of thought, Makarenko reported that

> I thought how full of hardship and injustice my life had been. How I had sacrificed the best years of my life simply that half a dozen "delinquents" might enter a *Rabfak*, how at the *Rabfak*, and in the big town, they would come under new influences, which I could not control. . . . Why all this injustice? Hadn't I done good work myself? . . . [Why do] I have to while away the dark night in a god-forsaken labour colony? (II, 208–9.)

Makarenko didn't come up with an adequate answer. And in these soliloquies he showed himself at his most human and his most troubled. In long passages such as these Makarenko is no longer confident and sure of the brave utopia that he is building, and he feels himself the eyeless toiler in the night. The troubling thoughts persisted, and when the notion of Kuryazh came up, he again clung to the hope that by reorganizing the colony once more he would have the chance to find the precious quality of the collective that still eluded him.

While on the crest of a wave, such as when inspecting the promising Popov palace for possible conversion to a new colony, Makarenko's optimism was boundless. At that time he was able to assert vigorously and confidently that

Perhaps the main distinction between our educational system and the bourgeois one lies precisely in the fact that with us a children's collective is bound to develop and prosper, to visualize a better morrow, and to aspire to it in joyful, common efforts, in gay, steadfast visions. Perhaps therein lies the true pedagogical dialectics (II, 297).

Yet when the Popov palace failed to become fact, his optimism in part deserted him, and he was left, in his darker moments, with doubts as to whether the collective was indeed an absolute. Makarenko found himself in the greatest possible uncertainty, and his usual practical intelligence failed him.

In making the decision to go to Kuryazh, Makarenko was

already showing signs of trusting, not in an explicit and conscious social psychology as his guide, but in intuition. Thus he began to consider that the truth of the fundamental nature of the collective, which he had hoped to demonstrate, had to be "felt" rather than "known." In allaying his fears at the move and at his failure to find the essence of the collective, he reflected that he and the colonists

did not so much know as feel the necessity of subordinating everything to the requirements of the collective, and that without any sense of sacrifice.

It was a joy, perhaps the deepest joy the world has to give— this feeling of interdependence, of the strength and flexibility of human relations, of the calm, vast power of the collective, vibrating in an atmosphere permeated with its own force (II, 334–35).

The departure for Kuryazh, with its desperate inmates waiting for the Gorkyites, was not the same confident affair that the departure to Trepke had been. Makarenko, with his gift for getting through to the essence of the situation, described it movingly.

After I had read them the agreement and the order, the Gorkyites did not shout "hurrah!" and did not toss anyone up. In the midst of a general silence Lapot said:
"Let's write to Gorky about it. And remember, lads: no whining!"
"Very good—no whining!" squealed a little chap.

And Kalina Ivanovitch waved his hand, and said: "Go ahead, lads, don't be afraid!" (II, 336).

CHAPTER 8

THE ATTAINMENT OF THE IDEAL

As had been stated in the last chapter, Makarenko saw Kuryazh as an advantageous site for at least two reasons: it offered him a chance to escape from the increasing pressure being exerted upon him by the orthodox educators, and it offered the challenge of a new environment, which was beginning to figure as an important principle in his educational thought. The fact that Kuryazh was physically repulsive afforded him no small pangs, and for some time prior to the departure he had qualms about it. Yet, when the "graduates" returned to Trepke from the Rabfak, they urged him to accept the challenge.

In appearance Kuryazh was filthy and dilapidated, the inmates were reduced to beggarliness, and their morale was completely undermined. The staff of the institution were incompetent and ignorant of the skills and attitudes necessary for the re-education of these children, and they themselves were demoralized as a result of their inability to effect any positive change. Yet the situation represented a challenge that Poltava and Trepke never had. Here, complete, was the material for a thoroughgoing application of the Makarenko method. At both Poltava and Trepke, Makarenko had been, as he freely admitted, groping blindly in a fog, searching for

113

any and every possible means of controlling the situation. But that had long since passed; the collective, with few faults, had been achieved. Already Makarenko had a sound, workable scheme that needed to be tested out in a totally new situation. The flaws that had been found, such as the failure of his method to win over boys like Chobot, or to eliminate completely such things as stealing, Makarenko simply saw as inadequacies of his knowledge and control systems, thus indicating need for further research. Kuryazh offered this and more.

Thinking over the challenge of Kuryazh, Makarenko marshaled in his mind the available knowledge of collective processes that he had already discovered. Primary in his thought was the concept of the structure of the collective, and in reflecting on his experiences of the past five-and-a-half years he decided to base his strategy on a rapid establishment within the colony of a strong, predictable organizational structure. Makarenko distrusted the ability of the boys to make the transition to a smooth organization by themselves. Although people usually desire the security of working peaceably and purposefully in society, in his opinion these children at Kuryazh, both boys and girls, were so completely demoralized that they would have to have the structure of group life thrust upon them. And the thrusting would have to be sudden; as Makarenko decided, "... I kept before me the idea of a single lightning stroke—the Kuryazhites must be taken by storm." * The danger of failure was very real to him, and he knew that his own collective at Trepke was by no means consolidated. Indeed, he was worried about any delay in absorbing the Kuryazhites into the structure lest the reverse happen and the Kuryazhites do the absorbing. Makarenko's notions of the need for a definite pattern is revealed in his thoughts on the eve of departure in March, 1926, when

---

* Makarenko, A. S., *The Road to Life*, Foreign Languages Publishing House, Moscow, 1955, vol. III, p. 9. Quotations in this chapter all come from this edition, and the volume number and pages are given in parentheses at the end of the quoted material.

he recorded that "... I knew very well that the best of boys can easily become wild beasts in a collective based on a flabby organizational structure" (III, 9). As Makarenko became increasingly committed to the notion, he realized that the impending struggle would serve a most valuable pedagogical purpose. If the struggle was successful—and here he saw himself as a general conducting a battle, an interesting analogy —then it would serve to make his collective stronger than ever. He pointed this out to one of the teachers:

> "The struggle at Kuryazh is necessary not only for Kuryazh and for my enemies, it is necessary for ourselves, too, for each one of our colonists. This struggle is of vital importance. Just go about among the colonists, and you'll see that retreat is impossible (III, 41).

In organizing the impending struggle, Makarenko had the entire staff of Kuryazh dismissed at the time of the transfer, and he sought fewer teachers, but more enthusiastic ones. The boys of the Gorki Colony were to remain at Trepke until Makarenko had thoroughly reconnoitered the position at Kuryazh, a process which took some weeks. Already it was clear in his mind that the Gorki Colony would have to have two aspects if it was to absorb the Kuryazhites successfully. On the one hand it would need an attractive appearance that would encourage emulation, and on the other it would have to be organized so tightly that disruption of its ranks would be difficult in the extreme.

At this stage there was no new thread of thought discernible in Makarenko's plans; in the Kuryazh episode he attempted to apply the methods that had already proved themselves to be successful. Nevertheless, Makarenko did focus his thought on the two salient features of the situation as he saw it—the attractive group appearance and the tight ingroup structure. In his search for these two features, Makarenko revealed that he was still very insecure in his knowledge of the ultimate qualities that bind groups together. The direction in which his thought was going is indicated in his musings over the problem in 1926 when, in going over in his mind the steps by which he planned to win the Kuryazhites, he decided that, first, "It was essential to try and pin down, if only roughly, any first signs of a collective, to discover traces of some sort of potential social adhesive" (III, 100). Again Makarenko revealed himself, as he did in his theory of finding the "nucleus," to be thinking as a social engineer, and already his thought showed signs of regarding the group as something to be constructed of individuals.

At the same time Makarenko had thought through the position to the point where he was prepared to assert quite emphatically that the besprizorniki were normal children who had become, in the euphemism of the day, "temporarily unsettled." He was prepared, on the basis of his experience, to deny any grounds for inherent depravity or moral defectiveness in the children. It was, of course, as much a part of his generally human and kindly outlook as it was of his knowledge or experiences. In the previous six or so years many of Makarenko's experiences were such that the temptation to dismiss these children as incorrigible was great, but to his credit this was confined to only a few cases, and they were, as is abundantly clear, the most limiting cases. Indeed, only once does Makarenko ever record that he met an incorrigible child.[1] Even more to his credit, it is clear that Makarenko's assertion of the normalcy of the besprizorniki is part of his own normative definition of them, an aspect of his idealization of the future Soviet society. If nothing else, Makarenko was distinguished through all of his life by an unquenchable desire to reassert the beauty of the morrow, no matter what the disillusions of the day. Kuryazh, more than any other moment in his recorded life, showed these qualities most clearly.

Whatever else Makarenko really harbored in the secret recesses of his mind, it is abundantly clear that he wanted desperately to believe in the future of his charges. In constructing his image of the besprizorniki, Makarenko made the most vigorous assumptions, including some that seem to run counter to generally accepted belief. For example, in asserting that the besprizorniki were temporarily unsettled, he denied that these gangs had any social structure of their own.[2] Thus he strongly criticized the orthodox educators for believing that

> the waifs were organized, that they had leaders and discipline, a regular strategy of thievish operations, and their own rules and regulations. They even honoured them with specific scientific terminology—"the spontaneously-arising collective," and all that sort of thing.
> ... All waifs were dubbed thieves, drunkards, rakes, drug addicts and syphilitics. Only to Peter the Great, in the whole history of the world, have so many mortal sins ever been attributed. . . .
> In reality, the life of waifs and strays in the Soviet Union was not the least like these anecdotes.
> The theory of a permanent waif society, filling our streets with its ideology as well as with its appalling crimes and picturesque attire, must be resolutely discarded . . . (III, 101–2).

The conflict of this attitude with the evidence comes out even in Makarenko's writings, and when he did find evidence to refute his above view, he then discarded the evidence resolutely. Thus, in the Kuryazh colony he wanted to find a normless collection of individuals to whom he could give a social structure; and when some structure was found, Makarenko discarded it as follows: "We did find certain traces of social adhesive substance in some places, but what it had joined together was not what we were looking for" (III, 100).

This sort of attitude shows how Makarenko was not looking for the real truth but constantly sought to arrange the situation so that it would be amenable to the sort of change and control to which he wished to subject it. Thus, in facing the task of organizing the debilitated Kuryazh colony, Makarenko saw the children as definite possibilities for re-education. As he stated it,

these children were by no means imbeciles, they were simply ordinary children placed by fate in the most absurd situation—deprived of the blessings of human development, and at the same
time removed from the bracing influence of the mere struggle
for existence by being given daily, if unpalatable nourishment
(III, 107).

The idealism and the worthy humanitarian motives that
inspired Makarenko to organize his perceptions in this way
must certainly win for him the admiration and respect of
those who have had experience with children of this sort.
And even those who have no more than a vicarious association with the besprizorniki, in whatever country and called
by whatever name, can hardly fail to appreciate the enormity
of the task that he set himself. Yet, at the same time, the way
in which Makarenko composed for himself a new way of
seeing old problems, and his idealistic disregard for patent
realities, posed problems which were to prevent him from
fully accomplishing his purposes. Thus, in the last quotation
above, he saw the besprizorniki deprived of the blessings of
"human development" and not, as most Westerners would
say, of "the home." For a concrete, tested reality, Makarenko
substituted a hazy, imperfectly understood ideal. Precisely
what Makarenko understood by the term "human development" he never said. Insofar as he denied the influence, beyond certain obvious elementary levels, of intrinsic factors
and stressed the primacy of the external environment, it is
clear that he could not, in talking of human development,
have meant any natural sequence of biological change,
whether it is looked at as unfolding, as ripening, or as natural
stage theory. Further, since he espoused quite vigorously the
environmentalist notion of personality, it seems that he saw
human development as a socially produced phenomenon.
The conflict of this sort of concept with his own thinking
becomes clear when it is considered that Makarenko opposed
any scientific study of the child which would be able to produce such a theory of social human development. From the

evidence available, it seems that Makarenko never adequately thought out this problem but rather glossed over it, confident in his own intuitive abilities in finding a way through.

Kuryazh stands out in Makarenko's career, then, as the place where the theory was tested in its entirety. At the same time it represents yet a further stage in the psychological development of his own perceptions and practices. With respect to the development of his particular educational methods, it is a final stage. However, it was by no means the end of his educational practice, and in the next chapter his work in the following decade will be considered; but it does, in a very real sense, mark the end of the period in which Makarenko evolved his specific educational methods to some degree of definiteness.

KURYAZH TAKEN BY STORM

According to plan, Kuryazh was taken by storm. The actual day-to-day events are fully detailed by Makarenko and although they can only be briefly touched upon here, the story is well worth reading. During the whole operation, Makarenko came through as an appealingly human character —at times rather too human. In response to the brazen insolence of the Kuryazhites in the early days, Makarenko's principles often failed him, and he felt an intense longing

to seize somebody or other by the collar coat now, this very instant, without moving from the spot, to rub his nose in the malodorous heaps and puddles, to demand immediate action—not pedagogy, or social education theory, not revolutionary duty, or communist fervour, no, nothing but ordinary common sense, ordinary, despised, philistine honesty! (III, 73).

The Gorkyites, in their usual fashion, marched triumphantly into the Kuryazh colony. At the head of the Gorki Colony were the colors, and then the military band, followed by the colonists themselves, their white shirts gleaming in the sunshine, "their bare legs swaying in youthful rhythm. . . . The only sound was the thunder of drums awaking a crisp echo which seemed to rebound from the far-off walls of Kuryazh" (III, 195). As the two groups of children drew up in opposing lines in the courtyard, Makarenko saw that the Gorki Colony had won the day. The assault had been successful.

Most of the younger ones were openly enthusiastic, just as they would have been about a toy which they wanted to get into their hands, a toy too exquisite to excite envy or stimulate vanity. Nisinov and Zoren stood with their arms around one another, regarding the Gorkyites; resting their heads on one another's shoulders, they seemed to be dreaming, perhaps of the time when they, too, would take their places in these entrancing ranks, and be admiringly regarded by small outsiders like themselves. . . . But the sarcastic countenances, got ready in advance, the sneering, scornful expressions—these were dissolving gradually. . . . Many of them were conquered on the spot by the splendid chests and biceps of the first of the Gorkyites. . . . Others were troubled later, when it became all too obvious that the very least of these hundred and twenty champions could not be touched with impunity (III, 199–200).

The story is most eulogistically told, and Makarenko writes as a proud father when his children become the center of public admiration.

In the succeeding days, the Gorkyites set about the task of getting the colony established. The Kuryazhites, impressed as they may have been with the first appearance of the Gorkyites, had as yet no cultivated habits. Makarenko realized very clearly that much of education is simple, continued habituation. The shock treatment was rapid, and it afforded the Gorkyites a chance to exercise their group solidarity. The Kuryazhites for their part were inducted into the new culture by any and every means available. They were stripped and disinfected, their clothing in many cases doused in alcohol and burnt, their heads were shaved and they were issued fresh clothing. In order to enforce discipline, they were refused food unless they earned it, and some of the bigger Gorkyites were not above manhandling to get their orders obeyed.

Immediately the whole four hundred children were organized into work detachments, and a daily regimen was posted. Makarenko sought wherever possible to get the children working, to get them actually physically involved in tasks, tasks which carried a definite reward on completion. Life proceeded according to the bugle calls that divided up the day. Altogether, the initial storming process took two months, from the arrival of the colonists on March 17, 1926, to the general meeting on May 15. On that day, the whole colony was called to a general meeting in which a manifesto was issued as the basis on which the colony was to operate in the immediately following weeks.

This manifesto was drawn up in secret conclave by the Gorkyites in their Komsomol (League of Young Communists) meetings, and it presented a thirteen-point program. These points covered three major aspects of colony life: administration, hygiene, and the work program. The original detachments were dissolved and twenty new ones, composed of members both of the original Gorki and Kuryazh colonies, were decreed. And as the collective authority, the commanders' council was confirmed in its rights. After considerable debate and argument, the resolution was carried in a wave of emotion and excitement. In two months, Makarenko had applied his system, and had pronounced it a success.

THE LIFE STYLE OF THE COLLECTIVE

There was no doubt that the success of the Kuryazh adventure confirmed for Makarenko the principle of applying a strong external form to a social group. This he espoused as one of the cardinal principles of his pedagogy, and for the remaining thirteen years of his life he relentlessly pushed this principle. From this time onward, Makarenko never doubted that the social group was an absolute and that the individual was but an aspect of it—one of the obvious symbols, as it were, by which the group is manifested. Individuality, for Makarenko, was an irregularity in the collective life, caused by a disruption of the normal human state, which is one of working peaceably in groups toward collective goals. Education, as he saw it, was the task of making the individual integral with the group. Of course, Makarenko freely admitted that he was working with a group that was highly disorganized and hence education for them was a clearly set-out task. The problem that worried him and that kept coming up time and again was a fundamental one. From whence did the group get its particular characteristics to which the individual had to conform? And in the case of a perfectly integrated group, what would be the function of education? Makarenko knew that his system of challenges had its best effects with people such as his besprizorniki, and in these last years at the Gorki Colony the problem of educating normal children began to figure increasingly in his thinking.

Characteristically, Makarenko was stimulated to work toward answers to these problems by challenges from the outside. Again he was attacked by the bureaucrats, for whom he was now showing an obvious hatred; in addition, his old doubts began to assail him. It is one of the most curious features of Makarenko's attitudes to Soviet life that he had a strong antipathy toward those in authority, and yet he constantly exhorted his charges to have respect for the great Soviet government. A highly feasible explanation of this conflict would be that Makarenko was prone to see the whole cast of his own actions in idealistic terms; the real world of bureaucrats, who wrote him annoying letters and paid him needling visits, he saw in another light—and the fact of this real world repelled him. Refuge was only to be found in a retreat to a self-constructed world of the ideal, and in this category belonged the abstract group of the "government."

Evidence to support this view can be found in the fact that Makarenko was to find, as later chapters will show, extreme difficulty in developing the concept of sovereignty in his charges to the point where they could appreciate that sovereignty was vested, not in Makarenko himself, but in another body, the body social. Indeed, Makarenko's method depended to a large extent on the force of his own personality and his representation of himself before the boys as a figure who was capable of battling the external forces of society; his success in having them identify with his own actions and thoughts was to militate against the colonists developing a sense of wider sovereignty.

In the case of criticisms against Makarenko, the chief ones at this stage were concerned with his application of external form. Thus, Varvara Victorovna Bregel, from the local education authority, criticized Makarenko one day in the following terms: "All your banners and drums and salutes— they only organize the young superficially." To this Makarenko replied with the following analogy:

"You seem to regard the young, or shall we say, the child, as a kind of box. There's the outside of it, the packing material, I suppose, and the inside—the entrails. You seem to think we should pay attention to nothing but the entrails, and yet, if it's not properly packed all those precious entrails will be lost" (III, 233).

For Makarenko the notion of external form was fundamental.

The elaboration of the rationale of this form occupied him for the next months, and gradually he emerged with a notion of duality. The external form acted in two ways to secure the desired behavioral changes. On the one hand it provided a positive framework within which the individual could get a ready basis of security and a justification for his actions; on the other, it provided an ideal pattern of behaviors toward which the individual behavior could be directed. Thus, as Makarenko came to see the problem as one of converting individuals to the desired courses of action, he saw that there must exist a definite framework within which the change could occur. This came, of course, at a time when Makarenko had got beyond the simple problem of merely getting the besprizorniki to act in broadly acceptable ways. Because he had come to accept the collectivity of man as the fundamental absolute upon which all life was premised, the problem of the individual figured even more greatly in his thinking.

A characteristic of Makarenko's thought was that he never explored the historic background of philosophical issues. On the contrary, as he preferred to ignore the past of his charges, so he showed a predilection to ignore the past of human history. In acting thus, he followed faithfully the then current Bolshevik ideal. Seeking no explanation of individual behavior in history, Makarenko instead seemed to have been content to work from the Marxist assumption that the previous history of mankind had been one of exploitation and was of relatively little help in guiding the course of future action. Indeed, as the brave new world was at hand, Russian thinking in education, as in all other areas, showed a tendency to disregard history as being of no use to the direction of change. When history was invoked it was invoked simply to assert the necessary historicity of the revolution itself and the new era.

Thus, at Kuryazh, Makarenko came to elaborate the theory of a *life style* in the organization of educational endeavor. This term subsumes his thinking about the externality of form, but it goes much further in its connotations and includes tradition, habits, *esprit de corps*, tone—in effect, it is a term used to cover the rich complex of activities, attitudes, and emotions that are part of any social organization. Thus he stated that

Style and tone have always been ignored in pedagogical theory, but in reality these qualities come under one of the most important headings in collective education.... The failure of many children's institutions may be attributed to the fact that they have created neither a style, nor habits and traditions . . . (III, 262).

In his opinion, if a life style exists in educational institutions, then the task of bringing the individual into harmony with the collective ideals will be greatly facilitated. Makarenko was careful enough to acknowledge that individual motives exist, but nevertheless the task for the Soviet educator is clear. Thus he wrote that "we still tolerate certain motives of personal satisfaction and self-interest, while persistently endeavouring to substitute for them the broader incentive of collective interests" (III, 258–59). Further, the life style can change individual behavior because of its mimetic attraction. In the case of the rapid conversion of the Kuryazhites, Makarenko attributed the success of the campaign in no small measure to the fact that the style of the Gorki Colonists was itself an attraction. As he wrote, "The decisive factor here was not even considerations of advantage, but, of course, collective suggestion. . . . [T]he Kuryazhites were unreservedly anxious to become members of the Gorky collective, just because it *was* a collective, and, as such, one of the hitherto untried sweets of life for them" (III, 259–60).

In bringing the individual into line with the life style of the collective, Makarenko still retained all of the caution that came from years of first-hand experience. The task of bringing the individual into the group was one that demanded care, patience, and an attention to detail. He is clear to state that he was "fully aware of the relentless law: there can be no simple dependency in pedagogical phenomena, here the syllogistic formula, the rapid deductive leap, are untenable" (III, 261). Thus, Makarenko was cautious about the application of external discipline, or of too frequent an application of coercion. Discipline, if it was to have any educative effect at all, had to be isolated, and it had to stand in distinct contrast to the rest of the behavior. Thus, in attempting to discipline a group of besprizorniki, Makarenko kept to the principle of only applying effort where it showed. In the cases of mass nonconformity, discipline would be "both difficult and ineffective, besides demanding much time, since a retributive measure is only of use when it removes the individual from the ranks, and is supported by the firm sentence of public opinion" (III, 261).

Despite the sagacity of many of his observations, Makarenko reported that the mastery of pedagogical technique still eluded him. "A true victory," he related, "required absolute mastery of pedagogical technique. I was just as solitary in the sphere of this technique as I had been in 1920 although I was not so comically ignorant" (III, 263). Makarenko still sought, as this statement reveals, to find the answers to his problems in an improved technique, and, in stating the position as he saw it in 1926, he was clear in his mind that it was still a failure of technique. Thus he ridiculed the contemporary efforts to find the true communist methods of education by allowing the child free rein—as many educators were doing. Under the influence of the most idealistic form of Marxism, those educators believed, as did Makarenko in his earliest days, that a truly communist society would be achieved by simply freeing people of the shackles of bourgeois conventions. It is an interesting observation that Makarenko consciously rejected this method with the withering statement that

The principal dogma of this creed [i.e., natural development] consisted in the statement that, given the aforementioned awe and respect for nature, the substance will inevitably develop into a communist personality. In reality the only things that grew under such purely natural conditions were what always does grow where nature is left to herself—just ordinary weeds: but this did not seem to trouble anyone—abstract ideas and principles were what the Olympians held dear (III, 264).

In this statement the Olympians were those who were currently finding considerable public favor for their educational work—men like Blonski, for example. Makarenko sought the answers in practical work.

The fundamental problem of Soviet education at that time, then, was one of making the individual a complete part of the group, of so identifying his interests and needs with those of the wider collective life that there would be no such thing as individuality as it was known in the West. From this position Makarenko moved on during his stay at Kuryazh to the elaboration of the underlying theory, although he was not to get a chance to implement it fully until a few years later in an altogether different colony. The elaboration of the theory came, once more, as an answer to a challenge to his methods. It must follow from Makarenko's position that he would not be too favorably disposed to discipline coming from within the individual. On the contrary, discipline for him, in its usual sense, was part of the life style or the form of the collective. As such, it was impressed through collective life.

DISCIPLINE AND THE INDIVIDUAL

If the collective is basic, then discipline must, in its nature, be concerned with the regulation of human conduct so that it will conform to the demands of the collective. As such, it will be, originally, in large part external to the individual. Only by a process of time will the individual be able to internalize these controls so that they operate from within the personality. In this respect Makarenko was working in fundamental contrast to his time, for in the late twenties "conscious discipline" was in fashion. Makarenko ridiculed this notion of a discipline that was supposed to come "from pure consciousness, from purely intellectual conviction, from the emanations of the soul, from ideas" (III, 265). After his experiences with the besprizorniki Makarenko had little faith in such a theory. Makarenko's aim was to rationalize discipline as that coming from collective experience and from the "friendly pressure" of the collective. Convinced that the collective was absolute, Makarenko wanted to understand and control the processes by which the individual could be willingly and positively brought under complete group domination. He rejected vehemently any deliberation in the selection of aims; these, he maintained, were known. The whole of life was simply the achievement of the socialist state. Thus, he was able to assert that in education "The problem, therefore, is not *what* is to be done, but *how* it is to be done. And this is a matter of pedagogical technique" (III, 265).

Makarenko's beliefs on this issue became so firm that he eventually considered the problem of education to be one of producing a given personality type, for only in this way can the complete harmony of the group be assured. His experiences with the besprizorniki, his denial of history, and his firm insistence upon the rightness of environmental conditioning led him to believe that human nature did not exist in any independent sense but only became realized as it was given form and meaning through the collective. Thus he came to the extreme conclusion that

it was clear to me that many details of human personality and behaviour could be made from dies, simply stamped out *en masse,* although of course the dies themselves had to be of the finest description, demanding scrupulous care and precision (III, 267).

The basic problem of Soviet education, in his view, was that of developing a technique of pedagogical engineering. Makarenko himself made no claims to have reached a solution, but he did feel that his methods with the besprizorniki were steps in the right direction.

Basic to the conscious application of discipline Makarenko saw the need for a conscious motivation. As the individual had to be consciously disciplined, so in like fashion motivation had to be external, or had to be "endeavor," as Makarenko termed it, and again consciously applied. In evolving his ideas on this subject, Makarenko came dangerously close to self-contradiction; certainly he came up with ideas that were somewhat incompatible, and in this respect he made himself vulnerable to charges of anticommunism. He saw that "heightening endeavor" had two aspects. Immediately, a system of incentives could be produced and, in longer range, the cultivation of higher collective goals could be sought. Of both of these he approved. The more immediate method, of offering incentives, he had found to work in the colony, and it became part of his educational theory. It is interesting to read his justification of incentives, especially ones such as wages.

Wages help the novice to learn to co-ordinate personal and social interests, he at once plunges into the complex network of the Soviet Industrial–Financial Plan, of economic calculations and evaluations, has an opportunity of studying the whole system of Soviet factory economics, and finds himself, at least theoretically, on a par with all other workers. Last, but not least, he learns to value earnings (III, 282).

More important than his theory of immediate incentives, however, is his theory of cultivating long-range incentives to encourage collective solidarity. This is the "system of perspectives" which Medinski, in the introduction to *The Road to Life,* praises enthusiastically as "remarkably profound" (I, 15). Makarenko turned to this because he was prevented from any widespread application of wages; as a result, he elaborated his beliefs on the fundamental values of human existence. In this period he came as close as he ever did to giving expression to his ideas on the purposes of human existence, and even in this he kept his gaze fixed on the future. He saw man as essentially oriented to the future. Thus, he was able to say that

Man must have something joyful ahead of him to live for. The true stimulus in human life is the morrow's joy. In pedagogical technique this not too distant joy is one of the most important objects to be worked for. In the first place the joy itself has to be organized, brought to life, and converted into a possibility. Next, primitive sources of satisfaction must be steadily converted into more complex and humanly significant joys (III, 282–83).

The purpose of organizing the joy in a collective form is so that the individual can conquer personal weakness and find strength in the future—a future which holds stronger promise of realization when it has the whole collective working for it. Thus, "The more comprehensive the collective with whose future prospects the individual is able to identify his own, the more beautiful and noble that individual appears" (III, 283).

When that became translated into educational terms, it emerged as the pithiest of all Makarenko's dicta: "To educate a man is to furnish him with a stimulus leading to the morrow's joy (III, 283). This epigram subsumes all of Makarenko's thinking and acting for the previous seven years, and from this point on his work took a new turn, a turn in the direction of re-examining his ideas so that his dictum could become the basis of Soviet education. Makarenko elaborated the dictum with the following words:

[Education] consists in the creation of fresh stimuli, in the full use of existing ones, in the gradual building-up of worthier ones. A beginning can be made with a good dinner, a visit to the circus, or cleaning the pond, but the prospects affecting the whole collective must be created and gradually widened, and brought to the point where they become those of the Soviet Union itself (III, 283–84).

Thus arose in Makarenko's mind the question of sovereignty. The new problem that engaged him was how best to effect the widening of interests once group identification was achieved. Secure in his belief that he had solved the problem of the identification of the individual and the group through the invention of the life style, the new problem alone remained. Then, at the moment he reached that point, a new train of circumstances caught him up and provided him with a fresh approach to the problem.

THE PROSPECT OF THE DZERZHINSKI
COMMUNE

Felix Dzerzhinski, the leader of the OGPU, or Soviet Police, had died in 1926, and as a memorial to him the OGPU
had decided to establish a model institution for besprizorniki. The model institution, situated on the side of Kharkov
opposite to the Kuryazh estate, was to be the last word in
architectural perfection; in typically Russian fashion, it was
to be built in an ornate style, complete with parquet floors
and painted ceilings. Makarenko was having a run of unusually troublesome problems, not the least of which was
that Vera, one of the colony's girls, gave birth to a child.
This brought no small amount of criticism on his head from
the authorities. Further, Professor Chaikin had made addi-
tional criticisms of Makarenko's methods. The police, for
their part, and not unnaturally, felt a strong sympathy for
the martial methods of Makarenko, and he was offered the
directorship of the new colony. Makarenko, a fervent ad-
mirer of the OGPU, found in them the very qualities that
he had long been seeking to cultivate, the chief point of his
enthusiasm hinging on the remarkable collective solidarity
that the police displayed. As Makarenko saw them,

the Cheka [3] collective was rich in those very qualities which I
had been trying for eight years to instil into the collective of the
colony.
. . . .
   At last I saw and felt for myself that precious substance for
which I could find no better name than "social adhesive"—that
feeling of common perspectives, that awareness of each other at
any stage of the work, of all members of the collective, the per-
petual consciousness of one high common goal, a consciousness
which never degenerates into mere pedantry and garrulity (III,
380–83).

By discovering such characteristics in the men of the OGPU,
Makarenko became even more secure in his belief that his
pedagogical scheme was the true Bolshevik scheme.

The final attack upon Makarenko that set the seal on his decision to leave Kuryazh for the new Dzerzhinski Commune came when Makarenko was summoned before the local education authority to explain his educational policies. Makarenko recorded that his theories on duty and discipline were strongly criticized and that even the concept of duty was derided as being bourgeois in origin. Chaikin, Makarenko recorded, denounced the idea in the following words: "Soviet pedagogics aims at cultivating the free manifestation of creative forces, inclinations, and initiative, but by no means the bourgeois idea of duty" (III, 400). After considerable debate, Makarenko was chastened with a unanimously passed resolution to the effect that "The proposed system of educational process is a non-Soviet system" (III, 403). This meant that Makarenko "began winding up the collective." On September 3, 1927, Makarenko left the Gorki Colony and assumed the full-time directorship of the Dzerzhinski Commune. An era in his life had ended.

PART III
THE IDEAL AND THE REAL

71

CHAPTER 9

CONFLICTS IN SOVIET EDUCATION

A DECADE OF BOLSHEVIK POWER

When Makarenko relinquished command of the Gorki Colony at its final location at Kuryazh and went on to direct the Dzerzhinski Commune, a decade of Bolshevik control had passed. During that period, Makarenko had been working with the besprizorniki for seven years and had evolved the fundamentals of his educational method. Although Makarenko was to live and work for another decade beyond this, he never made any radical or inconsistent changes in the methods that he had developed. In a sense, then, his creative work came to a close when he left the Gorki Colony. In point of fact, the exploratory phase of his work ended—he had solidified his rationale—and he began a totally new, analytical phase. For the next ten years he concerned himself with the logical analysis and application of his methods. In doing this, he dealt with the obvious realities of life in a way that his earlier methods had ignored. This logical analysis and application consolidated his earlier work at the Gorki Colony enormously and contributed to the growing reputation of his name. By the time that he died in 1939 his fame was secure and his methods vindicated.

The mere fact that Makarenko engaged in a period of theoretical consolidation of his achievements does not explain his success. On the contrary, his chance to engage in such work was dependent on what was for him a rather fortunate turn of events. In the previous section describing the process through which Makarenko evolved his methods, it was pointed out that he was constantly subjected to criticisms and attacks from other educators, and indeed the attacks became so strong that they forced him to move to Kuryazh, then to relinquish altogether his control of the Gorki Colony and to move under the protection of the Soviet Police. In understanding the rather rapid rise of Makarenko to fame it is important to understand the remarkable changes that took place at the turn of the decade.

For the whole of Makarenko's time at the Gorki Colony his methods were in opposition to those which were in official favor and, had the currently favored methods continued to remain popular, there is the strong possibility that Makarenko's name would have disappeared into oblivion and that *The Road to Life* would never have been published. As it was, in the years in which Makarenko worked in the Dzerzhinski Commune, the whole cast of Soviet domestic policy, and consequently that of education, underwent considerable change. It was fortunate for Makarenko that the direction of the change coincided with his own thought. To understand the manner in which Makarenko came into prominence, it is necessary to consider the development of Soviet education during the twenties and the manner of its change in the thirties.

THE YEARS OF EXPERIMENT

The phenomenon of Soviet education during the twenties is so remarkable that it is more than likely that it remains without parallel in the history of education. Anxious to implement the millennium in the shortest possible time—and doubtless convinced that it could be done—the Soviet educators, along with other social leaders, were unabashed in their endeavors to achieve the well-nigh impossible. The twenties and early thirties were years of conflict in Soviet education, and apart from the fact that Makarenko remained an unpublished author during those years and only made his major pronouncements well into the thirties, most of his success is due to the fact that his thought coincided with the new thought of the new era of the thirties. The fundamental conflict that Soviet education faced was the obvious one of reconciling the individual and the larger collective, ensuring at the same time that there was a steady growth toward the communist state.

The whole educational atmosphere was charged with the experimental attitude and the Webbs have analyzed it succinctly in the following words:

The whole decade, 1921–30, was a period of luxuriant experiment, when the lessons of other countries were ignored; discipline was neglected; the pupils were supposed to govern the school; the teachers did as they liked, whilst the inspectors favoured one system after another. The result has been described by foreign observers as a "joyous bedlam," in which the pupils learned all sorts of things, and the cleverest among them not a little, but seldom the formal lessons common to other countries.[1]

This was the position that came after the original platform laid down by Lunacharski on his assumption of the leadership of the new Soviet educational regime. Educational practices were to have the highest respect for the personality, and at the same time were to emphasize the labor basis of all human activity. The school was to become a true commune where experiences could be shared in working toward a common goal. To implement this, a coeducational, ten-year school was planned; the educational outcome of this was the new word which fell unfamiliarly upon Western ears at the time—polytechnization.

Polytechnization was something more than mere vocational training. It was a whole educational outlook which saw society based on shared, productive work and saw culture

as the sum total of this productive work. Thus, through polytechnization, through the production of cultured, complete
citizens, the Soviet educators hoped to achieve a nice balance
between the liberation of the individual and the necessary
cohesion of society. In a sense, the Soviet educators were
charged not only with the formal educational training of
children in basic skills, they were concerned with the actual
production of culture. The whole cultural tradition of the
communist era lay ahead of the people, not behind them.
Education became the instrument for inventing and keeping
in the public view the dreams or utopias.[2]

The obvious conflict that such a policy produced is evident
from writings of the time. Thomas Woody, for example, who
visited Russia in 1918 for several months and then spent a
year there in 1930, reports his conversations with Shatski, an
educator who in 1930 was director of a colony for besprizorniki, this colony being known as the "Colony of the Cheerful
Life." As the basis of his educational philosophy Shatski
brought out just such a picture—of the school as the creator
of culture.

Our aim is to build true culture. No nation has done so yet.
True culture must be founded on the good of all. School, educational philosophy and political life must all be united. No true
educational philosophy can be founded in a predatory society.
The uniformity and order of a disciplined, collective society is
better than the chaos and waste that are inevitable in a "free"
and individualistic one. To lay the educational bricks in building socialism is the high duty of current pedagogy.[3]

At the same time, Shatski saw no inconsistency in adapting
freely the educational ideas of John Dewey and, in effect,
developing them into a sort of Soviet "neo-Deweyanism."
Unlike Makarenko, who had a pronounced dislike for
America, Shatski claimed that no educational ideas from
Europe were, for him,

as significant or interesting as what came to us from America.
But, if Dewey and Tolstoi have exerted an influence, their idea

of "free education" is untenable. From my experiences I know that there is no free child; there is only a child, reflecting different training influences of environment. Therefore, behavior of the child should receive considerable social correction. It is here that we must correct the theory of Dewey.[4]

In the years that Makarenko was quietly working at establishing the first Gorki Colony at Poltava and inveighing against the lack of guidance from the educational theorists, the most obvious characteristic of Soviet education was the emphasis on experiment and testing. This was known as the "pedology" movement, and was especially championed by Pavel Blonski. Pinkevitch defined pedology as that science "concerned with the psychological and physical development of the child from birth to maturity. It studies the biology and psychology of human growth." [5] Under the stimulus of such men as Blonski, who was later to become discredited, the measurement and testing program grew apace until by 1926 he had tested the intelligence of 10,000 children in Moscow, and in 1927–28 had organized a program to measure the intelligence of every child entering school in two of the six educational districts of Moscow.[6]

At the same time that the pedology movement was in progress, the establishment of the school system was going forward. The one-track system of the labor school had been well established, and the curriculum, in line with the experimental notions, was organized according to the "complex" method, a sort of project system. Scott Nearing, who studied the Soviet system in the twenties, reported on the complex system in the following words:

Instead of beginning with books, they had begun with life—the life of the village in autumn. They were observing it, analyzing it, discussing it. The teacher read something about it from books. The children were not so far along. So they used the autumn for their books, studied it with great enthusiasm and in a month they had learned a great deal about the things that were happening all about them.[7]

Wilson reported that the complex method, by 1928, was all
but universal in elementary schools and existed in many high
schools, especially under the guidance of abler teachers,[8] in
which Nearing concurs, stating that he "did not go into a
single school where some form of it was not in operation." [9]
As well as the complex method, the Dalton plan was widely
favored.

In addition to such avowedly active methods of learning,
the schools were organized as centers of active pupil participation in the affairs of social and political organization. Children were encouraged to participate in school government, as
Makarenko encouraged his charges to form an executive
council, and a deliberate system of political party youth
groups was instituted, known as the Komsomols, or Young
Communist League.[10] These Komsomol groups were extremely effective in organizing the political consciences of
the children, and were especially championed by Lenin's
widow, Krupskaya. Thus in July, 1923, Krupskaya recom-
mended the Komsomol in a speech during Children's Week
because it

instils in its members collective instincts and accustoms them to
share joy and grief, teaches them to make the interests of the
collective their own, to regard themselves as members of the collective.... [I]t enhances children's communist consciousness by
helping them to realize that they are members of the working
class which is fighting for mankind's happiness, members of the
huge army of the international proletariat.[11]

In the *Teachers' Gazette* in 1927 she wrote that

the school and the Young Pioneer movement pursue one and the
same aim: to bring children up as fighters for and builders of a
new system. The goal of the Young Pioneer movement is to
bring up a new youth which will achieve socialist, communist
construction.[12]

The organization of Soviet education by 1927, a decade
after the beginnings of the new system, was an idealistic endeavor to have the total educative process geared to the twin

values of individuality and collectivity. Student discipline
was exercised through committees and through persuasion
of the community rather than through physical coercion, and
the organization of studies was based upon three broad "com-
plexes" of social life, bearing a strong resemblance to Kilpatrick's "project method." The whole of school life was
permeated with political ideals, and junior versions of the
Communist Party extended down into the schools. In theory
the entire nation was engaged in the transition from capi-
talism to socialism and was in the process of forging a new
and solidaristic society and a new socialist culture. The educational justification for such an organization of the educative process was that the desired learning outcomes

will be naturally acquired along the plan indicated, by the
methods of teaching applied to active work; if the school under-
stands how to profit by every occasion to permit the students to
put in practice—in socially useful activity—the theoretical
knowledge they have acquired.[13]

In all of this activity, there was much that accorded completely with Makarenko's own thinking and also with his
practice. The chief point at which he differed from the main
stream of educational activity was in his denial of the pre-
ciousness of the individual personality. It was not that Makarenko deliberately denied the individual, but rather that he
failed to see it as the beginnings of educational endeavor.
For Makarenko the individual personality was an obstruc-
tion to the attainment of the communist state, and he directed his efforts at the primary construction of the collective.
There is no doubt that Makarenko's actions were better
suited to the attainment of the communist goal; an idealistic
insistence on the rights of the individual personality was to
create enormous conflicts for Soviet educators. Krupskaya
sensed the enormity of the problem when she wrote in 1927
that "We should bring up our children as collectivists. How
is that to be done? Here indeed we have a serious pedagogical
problem."[14] In the same speech quoted above, Krupskaya

got to a clear understanding and analysis of the issues. Thus, she wrote:

The Soviet system of education aims at developing every child's ability, activity, consciousness, personality and individuality. That is why our methods differ [from the bourgeoisie]. . . . The bourgeoisie tries to bring up its children as individualists who set their ego above all else, who oppose the masses. . . . [W]e are for the all-round development of our children—to bring them up not to oppose the collective but on the contrary to constitute its force and raise it to a new level. We believe that a child's personality can be best and most fully developed only in a collective. For the collective does not destroy a child's personality, and it improves the quality and content of education.[15]

In such a statement by Krupskaya, the conflict is latent, and, as the years progressed, it became obvious to even the most ardent of the Soviet experimentalists that it would be impossible to reconcile both collective and individual education if it is already clearly postulated that a solidaristic, total society is the desired product. In attempting to go beyond Dewey the Soviet educators made a cardinal error. If nothing else, they completely misunderstood the nature of Dewey's experimentalism. The fact that they were able to prolong such a conflicting set of aims is explained by the fact that most Russian life was completely disorganized and that, for the initial years, the restoration of a simple order was mandatory.

The middle twenties were, on the other hand, a period of tremendous political struggle, and the issue of power was still undecided. Lenin died early in 1924, and it was not until Stalin triumphed over Trotski in 1928 that a new center of power was definitely established. Once that had occurred, attention in Russia began to be diverted to a re-intensification of efforts to introduce a complete and thorough-going socialist order. About 1927 the beginnings of educational change can be distinguished, and doubtless the change came as a coalescence of a variety of factors. The seizure of political power by Stalin on the one hand and the stabilization of the social order on the other were extremely helpful. But beyond that, as the schools became more consolidated, there was a gradual return to the older ways of doing things. Once the original burst of enthusiasm was spent, teachers lost their drive for the new methods and, in no little measure, their own creativity failed them. Many looked around for constructive guidance.

In general, the failure of the complex methods came from much the same reasons as the failure of progressive education in the West. As early as 1926 Nearing, during his visit to Russia, recorded a simple and obvious explanation of the failure of the progressive methods:

The "complex system," or unit problem system, succeeds very well for the first three or four years. The children like it, and the teachers are able to handle it effectively. Then some form of specialization becomes necessary because of the intricate nature of the problems that have to be handled. The old method was to let the child specialize—geometry, ancient history, physical geography, mechanical drawing. The aim of the Soviet school authorities is to keep classes at work on unit problems, but under the direction of a number of teachers who are specialists in particular fields.[16]

The growing failure of this method, as the mastery of organized bodies of subject matter became increasingly necessary, was paralleled by a failure of such techniques as the Dalton plan. On the same visit Nearing reported seeing a class at work and enquired of the principal: "Is this the Dalton Plan?"

The principal's answer indicates a clear understanding of the problem:

"No, we have abandoned the Dalton Plan. It produced too much individualism by setting up each student to do his own task. We want the students to learn group work. That is what they will be called upon to practice when they get out into the world." [17]

For these reasons, and doubtless for many others, after a decade the direction of Soviet education began to alter quite perceptibly and, before long, quite vigorously.

THE FORMALIZATION OF SOVIET EDUCATION

So far, Soviet educational policy had gone through two clearly defined stages—an early stage lasting but a few years following the assumption of power by the Bolsheviks, and marked by confusion and disorganization, along with a groping for a definite policy. This was followed by the "romantic" period of the twenties—in which the policy of "luxuriant experimentation" was adopted. Then, with the political triumph of Stalin, a new era began, characterized by a continued shaking off of one experimental innovation after another, and the gradual reintroduction of more formal—and frequently prerevolutionary—methods.

For a start, the change was not sweeping but, as Nearing reported, came slowly. The complex method gradually gave way in the higher grades to a more formal study of subject matter, and the Dalton plan was modified to what became known as the "brigade" system in which children worked in brigades of four, five, or six toward the achievement of group goals. In 1928, after a seven-year period of relatively free enterprise, the New Economic Policy came to a close and was replaced by the first Five Year Plan which had three major emphases. Its goals were the collectivization of agriculture, the increased development of industry, and the destruction of religion. The effects of this plan upon the school were immediate. It required the schools to improve and increase the output of technically-trained people who would be of use in the industrial fight, and it saw the inauguration of a systematic campaign to eliminate religion from the environment of the children.[18]

The first really prominent changes came in 1931 when

Andrei Bubnov succeeded Anatol Lunacharski as Peoples' Commissar for Education. Despite the apparent autonomy of each of the six republics, there was a high degree of conformity to the wishes of the central authority, and the decrees that followed in the next few years were rapidly implemented. In 1931 the project or complex method was finally abandoned; the modified brigade system of the Dalton plan was abolished the following year. By a decree of August 25, 1932, of the Central Committee of the Communist Party itself, the official pattern of teaching in the elementary and secondary schools was to be the "urok" system [19] and in the universities it was to be the "lecture" method.

There was a high level of uniformity in agreeing that the Russian methods of experiment in this decade had been wasteful, and one Russian educator stated quite categorically that "it had harmed a whole generation of school children, both intellectually and morally." [20] Curricula became fixed at the center, and a considerable number of reforms that had previously been considered bourgeois were introduced. Vladimir Samarin gives a clear concise account in the following words:

The standard lesson had been made the sole and mandatory form of instruction. Examinations had been introduced, as had a system of grades, ranging from "very poor" to "excellent," and later a numerical system ranging from "one" (lowest) to "five" (highest). Much greater demands than before were now made on the students with respect to discipline as well as academic achievement. Textbooks were widely used, and standard texts began to appear, one after another, in all subjects.[21]

The movement gathered momentum and increasingly, like a curious religious revival, testimony began to come in from all quarters on the hopelessness of the experimental methods as teachers and educators poured out their misgivings. The stage thus was set for the most influential reversal of the whole period of experiment when the entire scientific and psychological movement was officially dis-

credited. Thus it came as no surprise, and certainly as no
upset to the majority of Russian teachers, when, on July 4,
1936, the Central Committee of the Communist Party passed
the official decree banning the use of pedological methods in
the schools.[22] At this point the revolution had gone full cycle
in education and formal education had, in a sense, completely consolidated itself. The task now ahead of the Soviet
educator was to find a new method compatible with the new
position. Beatrice King, in 1937, reported that, faced with
"the task of discovering methods which should be adequate
to the demands of the cultural and economic life of the country," Soviet educators turned to this with a will.[23] Despite
the apparent return to the earlier bourgeois methods of formal subject-matter education, there was an important difference that made the Soviet educators unable to return
completely to old methods. The ideology of the revolution
was in no way changed, and the task was one of seeing that
education still fostered the socialist ideal and produced a collective spirit in the children. In so doing, the Communists
traded one conflict for another, for it is just as difficult to
utilize traditional subject-matter methods in the pursuit of
social solidarity as it is to use individualistic ones. For just as
the latter, to the Communists' obvious discomfort, led to the
production of independent neobourgeois types, so a traditional subject-matter approach can lead, if unchecked, to
independent thinking and intellectual dissension. The job
ahead for the Communists was to find a method of education
that cultivated essential skills and knowledge and yet at the
same time produced mentalities that were at one with the
party ideal and would lead to action in accordance with the
needs of group solidarity. It was in the methods developed by
Makarenko that one solution to the problem was found.

In the West, in England and the United States particularly, there was a mixed reaction to the Russian change.
While some saw it as a change for the worse, others were

more reserved in their judgments. In the United States, the change from progressivism to formalism was hailed by the conservatives as a victory for their side, while the progressives also claimed a victory. George Counts adjudicated the issue in an article in which he pointed out that

Each group has claimed at one time or another that Soviet experience has supported its position. Thus the progressives have maintained that immediately following the Revolution, Soviet educators examined the educational practices of the world and decided in their favor, introducing the Dalton method, the project method, free activity on the part of children, pupil government in an extreme form, and so on. The conservatives, while originally discounting this apparent triumph of progressive ideas in Russia, have more recently agreed that these ideas were weighed in the Soviet scales in the nineteen-twenties, as their opponents had maintained, but were found wanting. In support of their argument they point to the resolution of September, 1931, and to subsequent resolutions of the Central Committee of the Communist Party, which seemed to mark the deliberate abandonment of progressive methods all along the line and the restoration of discipline and authority in the school. As a matter of fact Soviet education, if examined fundamentally, is farther removed today from education in capitalistic countries, whether progressive or conservative, than at any other time since the Bolsheviks rose to power.[24]

Likewise, Beatrice King urged considerable caution in considering the apparently considerable change in Soviet educational policy. She argued that the changes were in great part due simply to the increasingly stable social order in Russia. Her observations led her to the conclusion that much of the apparently new order was simply a recombination of old elements, and that the Russians were simply reverting to their old ways in again insisting on a rigorous form of education. Hence she pointed out that "It is insistence on the improvement of quality that is the heart of the decrees. All else is subservient to this." [25] In addition, she observed that there was a new emphasis on the role of the individual. The direction in which the Soviet official thought was tending is interesting—emphasis on the individual was designed to exploit competitive desires and so raise production. Ten years later Lunacharski's emphasis on the rights of the individual were being officially endorsed. King observed that there was "the suggestion that individual competition be introduced to reinforce socialist competition." [26] There is no doubt from this article that King was decidedly in favor of a more tolerant appraisal of Soviet education, but her observations came three and a half years before the significant decree of July 4, 1936, in which it was made clear that individual values were not urged for the sake of the individual, but for the collective good. This was the period of the emergence of Stakhanovism, and of Stalin's new catch phrase, "Cadres decide everything." [27]

MAKARENKO AND THE NEW SOVIET
SYSTEM

In line with the emphasis on increased production, competition became an increasingly important element in the Soviet outlook. Thus, in an address to the graduating class of the Red Army Academy in May, 1935, Stalin said that "Technique without people who have mastered it is lifeless. But technique in the hands of people who know how to use it, can and ought to produce miracles." In the same speech, Stalin produced his new slogan, "Cadres decide everything" (Kadri reshayut vsye).[28] Whether by design or by fortunate coincidence, the following August his idea was perfectly exemplified by a coal miner in the Donets Basin, Alexei Stakhanov, who, according to Russian sources,

in one shift cut 102 tons of coal, although the normal requirement was 7 tons per shift. He thus exceeded the requirements fourteen and one-half times. Stakhanov thereby initiated a mass movement among industrial and agricultural workers to raise both production rates and output to new and high levels. In his honour, the new movement is known as the Stakhanov Movement.[29]

This occurred during the second Five Year Plan, and during that period the collectivization of the farms proceeded efficiently; the whole idea of Stakhanovism spread rapidly and, especially under the protection of the decrees of the Central Committee, spread into education itself. As the country became geared to ever higher production, and the need for a continued improvement in standards was felt, the schools responded by turning with more and more emphasis to systematized subject-teaching. The notion of the individual working for the greater good became more clearly promulgated, and the technique of the working cadres was implemented. This, of course, was precisely the method and rationale that Makarenko had hammered out for himself during his years at the Gorki Colony. Then he was alone and frequently attacked, and had had to suffer the bitter pain of leaving the Gorki Colony under censure from other educators. What Makarenko didn't know in those years was that his name, within the short space of a few years, would vault into public prominence. Suddenly, with the new emphasis, all of his ideas were vindicated: the "cadre," collective discipline, competition, and a concern on the part of each individual for the group's performance.

The times could scarcely have been more propitious for Makarenko. In June, 1927, he had been approached by the Soviet Police to supervise the organization of the Dzerzhinski Commune, and until October, 1927, for about five months, he supervised both the construction of the new commune and his other command at Kuryazh, the Gorki Colony. Then, on October 20, 1927, he took over full-time command of the new commune, a position which he held until July 1st, 1935, a period of nearly eight years, and longer in time than he spent with the Gorki Colony.

In 1925, sometime during the last months at Trepke,

Makarenko began to write the story of the Gorki Colony, the story which came to be called *The Road to Life*. This, however, was not published for some considerable time, especially since the times were hardly propitious for the public presentation of such an educational outlook. The first volume took a while to appear, and was not officially published until 1933, when it appeared in the magazines *1917* and *Soviet Literature*. This first volume of *The Road to Life* was praised by Gorki, who said that for him the appearance of *The Road to Life* was "a major event." [30] In August, 1934, the second volume was completed and sent to Gorki for criticism. Makarenko was working on *The Road to Life* while he was at the Dzerzhinski Commune and when he left there on the first of July, 1935, the third volume was still incomplete. He labored at it for the rest of the year, when the second and third parts appeared in the anthologies *1918* and *Soviet Literature*. The consolidation of the Stalinist regime was not yet complete, and the appearance of *The Road to Life* stirred up some considerable criticism, especially in the educational circles at the Moscow Pedagogical Institute, where he defended its thesis in public debate.

While he worked on *The Road to Life*, Makarenko busied himself with other works, and his literary output from about 1930 onwards was prolific. Toward the end of 1930, in October or November, he began to write an account in novel form of the Dzerzhinski Commune under the title of *The March of the Year Thirty*. This was followed by two more accounts of life in the same commune, *FD–1* and *The Major*, commenced in early 1932 and late 1933 respectively. *The March of the Year Thirty* (also known as *1930 Marches On*) was published in 1932, and *The Major*, a play in three acts, was submitted under the pseudonym of Andrei Galchenko to a national drama festival in 1933 where it was favorably commended by the judges. He wrote with increasing rapidity. Another play in three acts, *Newton's Ring*, was written at the end of 1934 but was never published. Articles on education, the first written with a specifically pedagogic intent, began to appear—in 1935 he wrote "Methods of Organizing the Process of Education" and "The Education of the People in the USSR." *The Major* appeared, still under the pseudonym, in *Literary Arts* in 1935. Following the death of Gorki in June, 1936, Makarenko wrote the pieces dedicated to his memory: "Maxim Gorki in My Life," "My First Teacher," and "Near, Dear and Unforgettable." In 1936 came the novel, *The Ways of a Generation,* and in the same year he began the greatest of his books since *The Road to Life,* a novel which sums up nearly all of his earlier writing —*Flags on the Battlements.* In 1937 he began writing the semi-autobiographical novel *Honor* and his third major work on education, *A Book for Parents.* This last was published the same year, in serialized form, in the two journals *Red Earth* and in *Literary Arts. Honor* appeared serialized in the magazine *October* in the November and December issues of 1937 and in the January, May, and June issues of 1938. Then, in 1938 *Flags on the Battlements* was published and appeared in issues 6, 7, and 8 of the journal *Red Earth.*

Meanwhile, as the educational climate became increasingly hospitable for Makarenko, due in no little measure to the rigor of the Stalinist oppression that reached full swing in 1937, he became extremely active in giving lectures to official bodies and gatherings of educators in which he expounded his views. In the four years after he left the Dzerzhinski Commune until his untimely death in 1939 he was solely occupied with writing, lecturing, and arguing his theories. From his obscurity in Poltava he became celebrated as a lecturer in the pedagogical institutes of such centers as Leningrad and Moscow; his ideas and methods became increasingly known in the Soviet Union and before long became models for emulation.

Most of his important lectures and articles have been collected together in Volume 5 of his *Collected Works* under the title of *General Questions of Pedagogical Theory—Edu-*

cation in the Soviet School; in general they are representa-
tions in more formal style of the views on education that he
presented in the three discursive, novel-type presentations of
The Road to Life, Learning to Live, and *A Book for Parents.*
While the theoretical works add little if anything to his educational theory and thought, they at least have the merit of
presenting the essentials of his thought without the didactic
style. Whether they possess any literary charm or style is, of
course, another question. There is no doubt that the novel-
type works do have a clarity and simplicity of style that in
itself is a recommendation, and I am inclined to think that
without the human context and the immediacy that these
books give, the theoretical works are, by contrast, rather dull.

Makarenko's thought, then, falls into two major periods.
The first period, produced at the time that he worked in the
Gorki Colony, and in the transition period of the Dzerzhinski Colony, was running contrary to that officially in vogue
during the same period. This thought is preserved chiefly
in the single work, *The Road to Life,* part of which was written while he was still at the Gorki Colony, and all of it while
he was actively engaged in the education of the besprizorniki.
Its hallmarks are immediacy, lack of sophistication, and a
dialectical exploration as Makarenko searched out the path
for himself, as an educator, to follow. Also to this period belongs *The March of the Year Thirty* and *FD–1,* although
both of these works are similar to *The Road to Life.* Fundamentally, in this period, Makarenko's thought is exploratory.

The second major period in Makarenko's thought came
toward the end of his stay at the Dzerzhinski Commune,
around 1935, and is marked by the increasingly analytical
cast he gives to the solution of problems, reaching a high
point around the years 1937 and 1938 with the publication
of *Learning to Live, A Book for Parents,* and numerous
speeches and articles. This is basically a period of logical
analysis.

In studying Makarenko's writings it is important to keep

these divisions in mind. It is also important to remember that all of his work appeared within the period of comparative safety afforded by the official suppression of opposing views. The later period, of course, is chiefly an ideal reconstruction of the past and, in a sense, Makarenko subjected his achievements to a historical treatment. It is with an examination of his thought in this second period that the next chapters are concerned.

CHAPTER 10

THE LOGICAL APPLICATION
OF METHOD

LEARNING TO LIVE IN THE DZERZHINSKI
COMMUNE

Once Makarenko left the Gorki Colony, he was finished with his creative period, and in the following years he primarily consolidated his thoughts into a system. Even the rough, improvised, unsuitable quarters and equipment of the Gorki days were gone forever. Whereas Makarenko was overwhelmed at Kuryazh by the stench of the place, which appeared to be "a complex blend of privies, cabbage soup, dung and . . . incense," [1] at the Dzerzhinski Commune an ultra-pristine atmosphere prevailed. Designed as a perfect memorial to the memory of Felix Dzerzhinski, no expense had been spared in its construction, and indeed so lavish was its final form that it invited critical comment. Makarenko reported in *Marsh 30 Goda* that

Many comrades reproached the Dzerzhinski Commune for having a palatial and even haughty style of living. Oh to dream of such a luxurious home! A home with parquetry floors, magnificent toilets, hot and cold showers, ceilings decorated with painted designs. . . .[2]

After seven years in the rough primitive camplike atmosphere of the Gorki Colony, there is no doubt that Makarenko en-

154

joyed such luxury—and the plumbing not a little. Here he was completely free to elaborate and perfect his system, free from supervision by the education department and free from the distractions of having to build toilets and supervise the kitchens.

In a way, he again went through the motions of establishing a collective much as he did in the Gorki Colony, but this time the drive was missing. Already he had, to his satisfaction, found the form of the collective, and in the Dzerzhinski Commune the immediate task was to apply the lessons already learned. What he attempted to do was to start this time at the top and work up. The contrast between the styles of *The Road to Life* and *Learning to Live* is quite startling. In the former he writes from the inside, as it were, as one concerned with the problems of daily life, battling, struggling, groping his way forward through the mists of ignorance and uncertainty for answers to the questions essential to keeping the colony in operation. In *Learning to Live,* however, Makarenko is distant, writing apart from the events that he describes. In this latter work he assumes the personality of one Zakharov and relates the events through Zakharov's eyes. The similarity bewteen Zakharov and George Orwell's Big Brother is too marked to be ignored.[3] Unlike the all-too-human Makarenko of the Gorki Colony who seized insolent youths in rage, who pitched in to help with the daily task, and who shared his meager supply of cigarettes with the boys at the end of the day, Zakharov is cool, aloof, omniscient, the supreme puppeteer, skilled in the arts of working others to his purposes, patient and tireless in his methods.

Nevertheless, considerable gains were made at the Dzerzhinski Commune. Makarenko devoted himself to the further investigation of three basic issues: the ultimate nature of the collective, the voluntary acceptance of the collective life by the individual, and the depth of impression that the external system can make upon the individual. In the new commune Makarenko was still dealing with besprizorniki, although

by now they were close to what in the West are called delinquents, the vast numbers of war orphans having passed beyond the need of institutional care.

At the time that Makarenko changed colonies, many of
the older Gorkyites were ready to go on to the Rabfak, while
considerable numbers of the others went out to work in industry and boarded in private homes in Kharkov. Altogether
Makarenko took fifty of the former Gorkyites with him to
the Dzerzhinski Commune in order to form, according to
the principles that he had evolved, a nucleus around which
the new collective could be built. This nucleus was to give
the life style to the new venture. The story of the development of the new commune is told in *The March of the Year
Thirty,* while its operations—with which the present chapter
is concerned—revealed and analyzed chronologically, are recorded in *Learning to Live.*

To develop the three main issues with which he grappled
in the Dzerzhinski Commune, Makarenko used the literary
device of following through the fortunes of different besprizorniki from their earlier lives in the streets through to the
Dzerzhinski Commune where their various reactions are recorded, analyzed, and eventually synthesized into a theory.
Although a variety of characters appear, there are three principal ones: Igor Chernogorski, Grisha Ryzhikov, and Wanda
Stadnitskaya. Initially their lives are separate: Igor is a clever
forger of postal money orders, Ryzhikov is a pickpocket,
while Wanda follows the oldest profession. Early in the story
they come together by chance, and later meet again at the
Dzerzhinski Commune, called in the book the First of May
Colony. Through their reactions to the colony and their various treatments, Makarenko traces out the method of his psychology.

In a sense, the three main characters are stereotypes and
represent not the complexities of individual lives so much as
simple, clearly drawn social problems. Even the use of their
given and family names is symbolic of their eventual situa-

tions. Igor and Wanda, described throughout by their given names, emerge as true Soviet types, while Ryzhikov, referred to chiefly by his family name, ends up ever a villain. At the same time, however, *Learning to Live* was written some time after the event and is, in itself, an idealistic reconstruction of the main issues of the past. Whatever its merits as an accurate analysis of what life really was like at the Dzerzhinski Commune, it was written toward the end of Makarenko's life, being contemporaneous with *A Book for Parents*. In this respect it represents the most definitive formulation of his thought in the last years of his life, and the simplification of the characters and the story at least possesses the merit of making explicit the basic features of Makarenko's methods and thought.

The fact that Ryzhikov failed to be absorbed by Makarenko's system is interesting in itself. Apart from the obvious honesty of Makarenko in acknowledging failure, it gives a clue to a fundamental error in Makarenko's basic assumptions. This was the assumption that the collective was the basic social unit and that the task of education was one of absorbing the individual into the group, of remaking the individual in the collective image. Igor and Wanda were good material for this, but Ryzhikov, like Chobot in the earlier story, failed to make the identification. The failure was seen as a failure of Ryzhikov, and even a failure of Makarenko, but never of the system.

THE COLLECTIVE: ASSUMPTIONS AND
FEATURES

The starting point from which Makarenko set out is given in an educational article written between the years 1935–36 in which he clearly indicated his belief in the necessity of developing the primacy of the total group structure. Thus he was aware that "A school must necessarily divide up into groups. There are obvious advantages in sectioning a school such as the facilitation of learning and the economical and maximum use of equipment and plant." [4] Yet Makarenko was aware that dividing a school up has many disadvantages, and in addition, such a concept of a school is insufficient because "education in such a form quickly falls away into small, narrow groups, and becomes apart from the questions of labour and industry, from the questions of the economic growth of institutions." [5]

In order to combat this, at the Dzerzhinski Commune Makarenko saw to it that the children, in addition to their school divisions and their dormitory divisions, were further divided up into work detachments of between seven and fifteen members, this number having been found to be optimum by previous experience in the Gorki Colony. These groups were so constituted that they shared rotating tasks, and in addition they came together for certain collective functions in which the solidarity of the whole collective could be manifested. [3] It is clear from this that Makarenko began with the original revolutionary ideal of keeping to the principle of education through productive labor.

The school was set up in detachments and had a pronounced military emphasis. The children, both boys and girls, dressed in a military uniform, consisting for the boys of riding breeches, boots and leather or cloth leggings, a belted tunic, and a visored cap. For the girls, a pleated skirt was issued, and shoes with stockings. A system of embroidered badges was employed, and an elaborate shoulder flash was the emblem of those who had been inducted into the inner circle and had the right to the title "colonist." This latter feature was an innovation of Makarenko's and is analogous to a formal initiation ceremony marking the end of an indefinite probationary period. Full membership of the colony, which brought with it a whole gamut of privileges, was dependent on a general vote of all the colonists who had themselves passed the probationary period. Like any troop, whether they be boy scouts or the grenadier guards, the commune had its special, highly embellished set of colors which was always under the care of a specially trained color party. To the standard were attached, in the manner of military regiments, emblems and other symbols of past glorious deeds.

The daily life was ordered according to a set of bugle calls; an involved system of ranks was instituted which necessitated salutes, officers-of-the-day, sentries, mounting guard, and carrying passes, like any army post. Above all hovered the set of regulations which provided for every contingency in the ordered life of the commune. Divided into two major parts, schoolroom and workshop, the whole day went according to posted orders. Even work in the industrial shops was organized in military fashion, and the "enemy" was underproduction. For each production period, quotas were fixed in advance, and then, in true Stakhanovite fashion, the detachments would set out in competition to beat the quotas. Each day's results were posted on the bulletin board. Thus, in the chapter entitled "The Bayonet Fight," the following bulletin was posted:

Our Red Banner right flank is in energetic pursuit of the defeated enemy. Today the girls reached the line of June 30, thus completing the plan for the second quarter of the year.

In the centre the metal-workers continue to exert pressure. Fulfilling and overfulfilling their program, the metal-workers reached the line of May 25, being today 15 days ahead of timetable.

The left flank remains halted on the line of March 15. But information received from the most authoritative sources (Blum) indicates that a decisive offensive is being prepared on the left flank.

Situation at the Front on May 12

The right flank, now engaged on fulfilling its program for the third quarter of the year, reached the line of July 3. In the centre, pressure continues to be exerted on the Blues. Today's engagements were fought on the line of May 29, 17 days ahead of time-table.

On the left flank there was uninterrupted artillery fire today —the carpenters are polishing a set of furniture.

Situation at the Front on May 14

After fierce bayonet fighting our gallant left flank destroyed
the Blues completely, broke through their front and are in active
pursuit of the enemy. The following trophies were taken: 700
lecture-hall desks, 500 drawing desks, 870 chairs. All prisoners of
war have been polished and delivered according to order. The
Blues are in retreat, our gallant carpenters today reached the
line of May 20 and stand today six days ahead of time-table. This
historic engagement is of great importance: the demoralized
enemy has fallen far back from the front. Our forces have lost
contact! Congratulations on your victory, colonists! *

By means of such an organized system, Makarenko felt that
the collective influence would absorb the individual, molding him to the group pattern. Theoretically, if Makarenko's
original assumptions were true about the essentially collective nature of man and the fact that all people want a simple,
ordered life, then the collective should, in a relatively com-
fortable sort of way, absorb the individual without any disturbing friction. Makarenko was not so naïve as to imagine
that the path would be so easy. All sorts of unaccountable
influences had entered into the lives of the besprizorniki
before he had control of them, and the induction was decidedly more difficult. In *Learning to Live*, Makarenko examined the various means by which this induction could be
made, using for the purposes the two characters of Igor Chernogorski and Grisha Ryzhikov. To study more closely the
means employed to bring these two persons into the group,
they will be examined in the two following sections.

IGOR CHERNOGORSKI: A STUDY IN SUCCESS

When he first entered the commune, Igor was openly defiant, and struck a characteristic note immediately with his
thought: "suppose I don't want to work" (p. 119). For Igor,

* Makarenko, A. S., *Learning to Live* (*Flagi na Bashnyakh*), Foreign Languages Publishing House, Moscow, 1954, p. 467–68. Quotations in this chapter come from this edition, and the pages are given in parentheses at the end
of the quoted material.

the system meant slavery, while his own outside life, for all its problematic quality, spelled freedom. Igor refused to work, although he accepted the privileges of food, clean clothing, and bedding. Beyond that, the commune had no effect upon him. After a few days, Igor was refused food until he worked, although this was in clear contravention of Soviet law, which Igor knew. Igor thus proposed formal complaint about his treatment, only to find that he had to lodge it at a general meeting of the commune. To his surprise they heard him out. This made an impression upon him. Thus, "On his way out of the building he found a certain satisfaction in putting his feelings of disapproval into words. How proud they were here of their regulations, their saluting, their badges" (p. 130).

The problem for the commune soon turned out to be one of presenting to Igor a rational explanation of the situation, and early in his days there this occurred. In conversation with Zorin, one of the colonists, Igor soon found out that he was not held at the commune under any form of restraint at all. Zorin pointed out that he could go if he pleased, especially if he thought he could do better elsewhere. This sort of challenge caught Igor on the hip, immediately putting him on the defensive. Thus he sought a reason for the form and function of the commune and put it to Zorin in this way: "but you haven't explained anything to me. What's the sense of it?" to which Zorin replied,

"The sense of it is that we need it. You've lived here two days, haven't you? You've been fed, haven't you? We've given you clothes and a bed. And there you were in the dining hall today already shouting: 'You've no right to do this!' And why haven't we the right? You think it's no business of yours where all we've given you comes from!" (p. 145).

The conversation then went on with Zorin pointing out that any individual's success came as much from the social situation and his fellows as it did from individual initiative. Already the beginnings of doubt had been sown in Igor's mind, and he sat down after the conversation to think it over.

Of course, Igor had not been convinced by [his] words but he no longer felt like arguing with him, while a simple and easily attainable desire had arisen in him: why not try? He felt ready to put a certain amount of trust in these people (p. 147).

The influences of the colony began to seep into Igor. One night in the dining hall, Igor pondered the question and

had to admit, [that the colony] formed one friendly family, close-knit, and proud of its community spirit. What especially appealed to Igor was the fact that he had not noticed in all these four days a single quarrel or row, not even a difference of opinion, or an angry or quarrelsome tone of voice worth mentioning (pp. 166–67).

This collective solidarity was to work against Igor, however, as he soon found out. He made an attempt to work, but this failed because he thought that the task, polishing chair struts, was meaningless. Summoned before a meeting of the Commanders' Council, a vote was taken on how to deal with him, one of the proposals having been to expel him. Before the result was taken, a worrying thought seized Igor. " 'They may really chuck me out, it seems!' flashed through his mind. And suddenly he felt unusually alarmed" (p. 175).

The problem, as the Commanders' Council decided, was not one of expelling Igor, but of the voluntary acceptance of the collective ideals. The dilemma was neatly expressed by Grinhaus—" 'We can't chuck him out, . . . but, of course, we can't put up with his behaviour' " (p. 177). Eventually, Makarenko himself, as the character Zakharov, took the matter in hand and made an eloquent, rational analysis of the situation. The basic appeal lay in the isomorphism between the individual and the collective:

"Man cannot live on his own. You've got to learn to love the collective, get to know it, find out what its interests are, and share them. You can't be a real man without doing that. Of course, rubbing down struts isn't interesting to you personally just now, but it's in the colony's interests and that means you've got to make it your interest too" (p. 182).

This marked the beginning of Igor's merging with the group. Returning to his task, he gradually became taken up with the success that he enjoyed in getting closer to meeting his quota. As the others praised him for his success, Igor slowly came under the spell of belonging to the collective. As time passed, Igor underwent subtle change, and it affected him profoundly to discover that other people cared for him, especially his class teacher, who commended him for a good composition. Igor became caught up with success, and became more and more deeply identified with the group, until he became a detachment commander, and eventually secretary of the Commanders' Council. As Makarenko recorded, "Somehow he failed to notice the exact moment his character had changed" (p. 485).

Igor brilliantly vindicated, to Makarenko's satisfaction, the truth of the collective principle. All that was needed was a rational analysis and explanation of the position, along with the friendly pressure and encouragement of the collective. In addition, the actual structure helped, with its ordering of the steps by which progress through the colony could be made. Failure, however, also hung on Makarenko's efforts, and the case of Ryzhikov illustrated this rather clearly. In addition, it gave rise in Makarenko's mind to certain doubts and misgivings that had not hitherto been felt.

GRISHA RYZHIKOV: THE FAILURE OF THE
COLLECTIVE

Ryzhikov illustrates another type of person with whom the collective had trouble—the type that assumed all of the external forms without the inner spirit. In Ryzhikov's case, he appeared to be a perfectly integrated member of the collective once he found himself at ease within the new situation, and for a considerable period of time he was actually con-

sidered to be one of the best workers. Ryzhikov rose to become, with misgivings on the part of some, a detachment
commander. In manner and demeanor, he was exemplary,
and never in his actions gave cause for suspicion. Yet, while
this was occurring, Ryzhikov indulged in an organized campaign of stealing, especially of goods such as watches and
precision-shop tools, which he could sell in questionable
shops in Kharkov. In addition, he also stole for the purpose
of casting suspicion onto others in the commune. For quite
a while he was successful in throwing the colony into confusion, and at times the whole soundness of the collective
structure was endangered because of the element of doubt
that tinged the actions of most of the colonists.

As Ryzhikov became emboldened with success, he came
close to arousing censure, as, for example, when he was discovered coming home late one night from the town, drunk.
The immediate response, under the guidance of Makarenko,
was to treat this as a failure on the part of Ryzhikov to become completely habituated to his new surroundings. Thus,
in pleading on his behalf, Volenko said:

"We ought to realize that Ryzhikov has grown used to living
that way. . . . He can't make a sudden break with his past. We
must wait, comrades. There's no sense in punishing him. He
doesn't understand anything about punishment yet. But you'll
see, you'll see" (p. 407).

Later, when Ryzhikov stole two overcoats, Makarenko said,
not knowing who the culprit was, "It's simply someone who's
still got the habit" (p. 421).

Nevertheless, individual guilt was felt as collective guilt,
and the whole collective suffered through the actions of the
unknown thief; as Makarenko reported, "The collective
spirit of the detachment was broken" (p. 547). Suspicion fell
in turn on everybody, everybody watched everyone else, the
whole of the colony became infected with the restlessness of
uncertainty. The manner in which the collective solidarity
broke down when the suspicion of guilt fell upon each mem-

ber in turn gave rise to an interesting description of a collective in process of foundering. Tensions rose, suspicions came thick and fast, evidence pointing now to this member, now to that, was offered. Tempers frayed, arguments became more frequent, demands for explanation were made increasingly.

The scene at the eventual unmasking of Ryzhikov is an astonishing account of the wrath of the collective when a real object of guilt can be found. Two boys, working in concert, discovered Ryzhikov at work and reported their discovery to the Commanders' Council. He was seized by the scruff of the neck and flung into the center of the room, falling to the floor with such force that when he rose his mouth was bleeding. The questioners, eager-eyed, shot one question after another at him, and

the fact remained that after he had told his tale there was not a mystery left unsolved. The overcoats, the [theatre stage] curtain, the silver watch, tools of all sorts, all kinds of incidents were cleared up. It was he who put the wrench in Levitin's locker. Twice he had set fire to the old "stadium." Ryzhikov told his tale in a monotonous woe-begone voice, exaggerating nothing, adding no embroideries, but not neglecting to blink and grimace (p. 627).

Ryzhikov was a problem that the collective failed to solve, and Makarenko had to resort to a tested method—he sent for the police, and it was they who took Ryzhikov away for further treatment. Thus, in such an extreme situation as this, Makarenko's system, like all others, had to fall back upon expulsion. After Ryzhikov had gone, the colony regained much of its former spirit, and Makarenko echoed a group sentiment when he said that "To many it seemed as if all that had passed was a dream, that Ryzhikov had never existed, that the colony had never known sorrow in all its existence" (p. 633).

Despite the experience, Ryzhikov hovered in the memory of the collective, and Kreutzer, the policeman, warned them in a solemn speech that

"now you know what an enemy is and how much harm he can
do. Your enemies will never come to you in a colourless and dingy
guise. They will always seek to dazzle your eyes and worm their
way into your heart. They will try to make themselves popular,
do all kinds of things for you so that you will consider them your
comrades. You have had a good lesson but you must keep a careful look-out.... Keep your eyes skinned in future too, discrimi-
nate correctly. It's essential for your own sake and for the sake
of your Soviet country!" (pp. 633–34).

Makarenko thus laid the foundation of the principle of institutionalized suspicion, such principles being taught in all
Soviet institutions after 1935.

A METHOD FOR PRODUCING THE NEW
SOVIET MAN

If the production of the new Soviet man was Makarenko's
aim, as he declared it to be, then in *Learning to Live* the
most definitive account of his success is to be found. The
stories of characters like Igor and Ryzhikov exemplify the
fundamentals of his method. Never deviating from his belief
in the necessity of first structuring the group, Makarenko
urged this as a cardinal pedagogical principle to the end of
his life. To that had to be added the principle of developing
and maintaining a strong in-group cohesion with an almost
ruthless disregard for transgressors of the social norms. With
such an emphasis on the power of environmental molding,
the individual past of each person mattered little. What did
matter was the need to provide a clear system of relationships
so as to provide a ready basis for security for each person; but
in return complete loyalty to the group and a recognition of
its primary claims had to be rendered. Beyond this, the collective had to have a motivation that came as an external
challenge, symbolized by the concept of Stakhanovism.

The translated title of the book, *Learning to Live,* is indicative of Makarenko's method and, when read in context,

it becomes clear indeed. Thus, in a speech to the colonists toward the end of his stay at the Dzerzhinski Commune, Makarenko summarized all of this into a paragraph:

"The First of May Colony has been in existence nearly seven years. Like you, I am proud of our colony. Our collective has great strength and lots of intelligence. Our future is rosy. At the present time we have 300,000 rubles to our current account. We shall be helped by the state because we deserve help. We love our state and are honestly doing what our country requires us to do: learning to live like real Soviet people" (p. 308).

The last phrase is of the utmost importance, containing as it does the essence of his thought. As a description of what actually went on in the Dzerzhinski Commune, or in the Gorki Colony, it is completely inaccurate. It is a normative and not a descriptive definition.

In the normative nature of Makarenko's vision can be found an explanation for much of his activity and, at the same time, the source of many of his problems. By contrasting his colonists with the rest of Soviet society, and by picturing the true Soviet society as a utopian future state, his educational theory was essentially a limited theory, applicable only to a small group for a definite, limited period of time. It is abundantly clear that Makarenko was not concerned with getting children to learn to live as Soviet people really are, but with Soviet people as they ought to be, in his own view. In immediate terms, his efforts were not so unsuccessful as might be imagined. For, in this period—around the year 1937—the Soviet Union, with the purges of the Stalinist terror, was rapidly becoming a totalitarian state, and the vision of the eventual state control of all aspects of all lives would be extremely accommodating to Makarenko's views. Due to this, many of his charges were able to go out into a limited area of society where their specific training would be eminently acceptable. Many of them went into further limited, highly organized situations such as the armed forces, the brigades of collective farmers or workers, and the Rabfak.

In situations such as these, their training in the colony would be a decided advantage.

Yet Makarenko was aware that much of his work was not meeting the requirements of the situation as it really was, and his thought was to concern itself, for a brief period, with the problem of education beyond the colony, with the problem of coming to grips with a reconciliation of the ideal and the real. Thus, despite early attempts to suppress it, the family still remained a strong institution in Russia, and Makarenko had to revise his views of society in order to include it. Likewise, he found that such notions as romantic love were not to be easily discarded. Conventional morality he found difficult to do away with altogether, especially in such matters as pregnancy among the girls. To these problems he addressed himself, as the power group within the party itself had to, once it became evident that a completely new society was not going to eventuate. Beyond these fundamental issues, Makarenko remained bothered with such problems as the ultimate nature of the individual, and the area of the completely private and personal, which he had not hitherto allowed for. Discipline, which in his view was the ability "to do things that are unpleasant, onerous, difficult" (p. 309), had to be reconsidered, although he found it impossible to effect a change in this notion. The closest that Makarenko ever came to a conscious explication of the sovereignty of the individual was in a thought he had that children are more than "objects for education" but are "living their lives" (p. 199).

The failure of the group to accommodate Ryzhikov troubled him considerably and he reported to a meeting in Leningrad that Ryzhikov was "not a conscious wrecker but some sort of vermin by nature. . . . [He] could not become assimilated even into our community." [7] A denial of the power of environmental conditioning is strange for Makarenko, and it indicates the extremes to which a person like Ryzhikov tested and strained the system. Makarenko promised to deal with the problem and "one day I shall write a long and serious book about it, a book on the methods of communist education" (p. 646). That day never came.

Despite these problems, *Learning to Live* demonstrates his faith in the principle that there are seldom such people as moral defectives and that, "if a child goes wrong, it is not the child who is to be blamed but the method of education" (p. 647). In this vein, he thought hard about the problem of the family and the child who is dependent chiefly for moral education upon the home. Here he saw the great danger to his theory of a wide collectivity, for the family represented a challenge to complete national solidarity. This in a sense was a dilemma of Makarenko's: how to educate according to his methods, and yet at the same time get a transfer of allegiance to the wider collective—how to instill the notion of the greater sovereignty of the nation. To this problem he addressed himself in *A Book for Parents*, where he came around to the notion that the family can be part of the Soviet system if it is thought of as a collective itself—that is, a family with enough children to form a collective. He himself expressed the challenge that the family offered him. Thus he said that "Children with families are a thousand times more difficult to teach than street waifs. The waifs had nobody else but me while school children always have a father and mother behind them. For that reason I'd very much like to teach normal children" (p. 648).

Learning to Live is a revealing study of his method logically applied. Within its limited situation, it worked admirably. In controlling children who were on the very margin of society and in giving them a strong sense of security and belonging as well as a vision of the future, Makarenko was eminently successful. Considered in the context of the society at the time, there is no doubt that his methods were more than acceptable; and it is easy to see, with the rapid acceleration of Russia toward the concept of the total state, why his methods should be so acclaimed. Whether Makarenko developed an educational theory of any universality or of applicability beyond the particular system, and whether his method was to be productive, is a question to which we must now turn.

CHAPTER 11
TOWARD THE TOTAL STATE

THE ACCEPTANCE OF THE FAMILY

In *A Book for Parents* Makarenko developed the second
phase of his life work into a final statement. Along with
Learning to Live it gives the reflective, rationalized aspect
of his educational practice. Not long after the publication of
A Book for Parents, Makarenko died unexpectedly in a train
while returning to Moscow from a nearby writers' rest home
in the country.

In a sense, *A Book for Parents* represents a full cycle in
Makarenko's thinking, insofar as in it he gives expression to
his belief in the need to include all of extant society within
the framework of the normatively constructed ideal Soviet
society. In the early days of the Gorki Colony, Makarenko
based his practice upon the exclusion of the outside world,
but the limited nature of his theory became apparent to him,
and in the final years of his life he recognized the need to
provide for the whole society. To do this, of course, entailed
the recognition of the family, and as this had been previously
denounced as a bourgeois institution, it was necessary to examine closely the nature of the family, its social function,
and the source of its authority.

The need to recognize the family had a dual motivation.
On the one hand, it seemed rather conclusive that the family

171

was a fundamental form of human social organization since it had persisted through all of recorded history despite the vicissitudes of the times—and this notwithstanding the fact that it had lost much of its economic basis and had moved to the more specialized function of providing psychological security. On the other hand was the negative but equally pressing fact that there was no possibility of any other form of social organization being adopted. As it was, the provision of the camps for the besprizorniki had strained the economy severely, and any attempt to extend such forms of communal living was completely out of the question.

Clearly the continuation of the family in its bourgeois form would be inimical to the continued growth of the true Soviet system, and yet a solution had to be found. At the very time that a definitive statement was needed upon the nature and function of the family in Soviet life, Makarenko came up with what was in effect a very neat, cogent answer to the problem. The answer came, not from any prior philosophical quest for an understanding of the nature of the social world, but from an attempt to round out inadequacies in his own educational thinking, from the need and desire to make his educational theory as complete and universal as possible. Because of this, Makarenko's view of the family is an educational one. He saw the family primarily as an institution within which the education of the child proceeds. As Western theorists do, he would want to include among the functions of the family such things as the provision of psychological security and social experiences and retain the family as a point of reference from which the world is psychologically constructed, but these were kept incidental and subservient to the overwhelming function of providing the necessary experiences for the complete collective education of the Soviet man.

While the school and the home are generally considered to supplement each other, there are many points at which they repeat experiences and overlap each other's functions. Nevertheless, it is usually possible to separate the types of experiences that the home and the school provide. For Makarenko, the separation was not clearly made. In contrast to Western practice, where the home emphasizes moral growth and the school concentrates upon intellectual, he wanted to keep both the school and the home concerned with the overwhelming purpose of fostering collectivity. There is no doubt that Makarenko would have preferred to have found some other solution to the organization of social life; his misgivings on the family were considerable. Thus he was never willing to entrust to the home exclusive rights for the provision of any particular experiences. If any institution was to have exclusive rights, Makarenko would have preferred it to have been the school. As things are in this modern age, the school in all industrialized countries has a virtual monopoly over the provision of intellectual and vocational experiences. That these functions were proper to the school Makarenko never denied, but for him they were not the primary functions. The school, like the family, he argued, existed primarily for the social purpose of providing a common collective consciousness; each was to reinforce the other in the cultivation of this consciousness.

Underlying his whole theory was a belief in the need for positive social direction. Imbued with the Marxist doctrine of the reconstruction of society, Makarenko saw both the family and the school as instruments for the achievement of social direction; at the same time he saw them as parts of that greater, all-embracing instrument of social direction—education. For Makarenko, education was the supreme instrument for achieving the new society. In contrast to the early days of communism, when education was not particularly singled out, in his writings education became the key means for achieving the desired social ends. The very opening paragraph of *A Book for Parents* sets the tone of what is to follow: "In moulding their children, modern parents mould the future history of our country and, consequently, the history of the world as well." *

The task of achieving the total society, one in which all aspects of the individual's life are regulated by the state, is difficult to implement. In the case of Soviet Russia, there was no possibility of starting from the ground up with the whole society as Makarenko had done with a part of it at the Gorki Colony. Instead, the new structure had to be erected on the old foundations, and this meant that a considerable amount of old belief, culture, and even simple habits had to be tolerated, at the beginning. Russian methods of child training had always been rather child centered, and the recent upheavals in all aspects of life had done nothing to make them in any way more authoritarian. *A Book for Parents* came as Makarenko's first and, as it turned out, last attempt to deal with the problems of home upbringing. As the psychological movement in education had lost much of its force in this period, and as psychological evidence of a strictly scientific nature was not always amenable to the production of the Soviet type, there was considerable need for books dealing with techniques for producing the new type. Pedagogues, parents, social workers—there were many who sought specific guidance and leadership in the task, and for them *A Book for Parents* was written.

A Book for Parents is considerably different from *The Road to Life* and *Learning to Live*. It consists mainly of a collection of parables and moral stories concerning various problems of family relationships. In some cases the stories are very short, some little more than a page; others, such as the account of the Vetkin family or of the deserted wife, Yevgenia Alexeyevna, or the little boy Timka, occupy up to fifty or sixty pages. The parables are not always of bad deeds

* Makarenko, A. S., *A Book for Parents* (*Kniga dlya Roditelei*), Foreign Languages Publishing House, Moscow, 1954, p. 7. Quotations in this chapter come from this edition, and the pages are given in parentheses at the end of the quoted material.

with suggestions for cure: often they are of good deeds and good families and are intended to point up the positive and desirable features of Soviet family life. The story of the Vetkins, for instance, is intended to show how delightful and purposeful life in a large, even though poor, family can be if only the true collective spirit is there. Frequently the stories are arranged in groups, or in balanced pairs, one illustrating the negative and the other the positive aspects of the same situation. Interwoven with the stories is a commentary, psychological in nature, intended to explain the processes as they are worked out in action. Frequently Makarenko indulges in a psychologization of the processes, at other times his concern is to make the interpretation normative and idealistic.

Formed into nine untitled chapters, there is no clear pattern by which the work progresses. Makarenko gives neither a table of contents nor an index. The clue to the organization is given toward the end of the book in a quotation from Felix Dzerzhinski.

"I am no ascetic; but the feelings must develop dialectically." [1] The whole series of stories forms a dialectic progression rather than a logical or systematic one; they are so arranged as to develop the concepts as they would arise in an attempt to take the immediately felt problems and to push them back to their ultimate foundations. The stories themselves come from Makarenko's own experiences, many of them from experiences had while living in the colonies for besprizorniki, others from his life since then. The dialectic progression is Makarenko's, not the readers, although they are arranged so that the reader is able to identify his problems with Makarenko's. It is an attempt to find a pattern of consistent, coherent meaning in the world, and at the same time to find in this world a pattern that contains the essential elements of the collective system so that it could be brought under control.

Within this framework, however, there is discernible a

definite sequence. In general, Makarenko deals with four
problems, although these overlap considerably and are not
completely self-contained. They do form a rough sort of
sequence; in order, they are the argument for the family, the
form of the family, the organization of the family, and the
purpose of the family.

THE ARGUMENT FOR THE FAMILY

The argument for the family is quite simply put. Basically,
to Makarenko society was a single, indivisible whole, thoroughly monistic in nature, and admitting in theory of no
basic division. The divisions that occurred were simply those
of necessity, necessary in order to get the work of the world
done. Whenever a division occurred that seemed to be inimical to the whole society, as in Makarenko's opinion was the
bourgeois family, he strove to eliminate any grounds for exclusion and instead sought to find an isomorphism, or identicality of structure, between the whole and each part. Thus
he asserted that the family "is an organic part of Soviet society, and every attempt it makes to build up its own experience independently of the moral demands of society is bound
to result in a disproportion, discordant as an alarm-bell"
(p. 51).

The bourgeois family for him was an infelicitous social
form that had no real basis in human life, existing in order
to work against fundamental human purposes. For Makarenko, man is born into a social life of great love which has
for centuries labored under the oppression of certain domi-
nant people who have prevented the full flowering of this
love. Dominance is produced by certain pathologies of life,
and in social life is shown as greed, the chief characteristic
of bourgeois society. Organized to cultivate greed, the bourgeois family is actually working against the best interests of
society as a whole, and as such has no real place in the social

order. For Makarenko the only good society is the socialist society in which the sharing of everything produces the necessities of life for all, thus allowing each person to develop both fully and freely without hindrances created by want. The family, therefore, in a socialist society, is a natural subdivision of that society seen as a whole. Naturally, the development of the individual must be in the direction of achieving a complete identicality of interests with that of the wider society, and in this the family can play an important role. The family assists in the educational process.

The need for the family is further clearly brought out in Makarenko's recognition that the individual cannot be educated apart from social groups for most of his waking hours. Certainly it is a physical as well as a collective impossibility, in addition to being undesirable, for a person to be educated by only one other person. Makarenko realized that fact and made it clear. Thus he indicated that

A Soviet person cannot be educated by the direct influence of one personality, whatever the qualities this personality may possess. Education is a social process in the broadest sense of the term. Everything contributes to education: people, things, events, but first of all and above all—people.
. . . .
[And] it is the family, or, if you like, the parents that are responsible for the child's upbringing (pp. 18–19).

Through the family, the individual can be developed into full collective consciousness, especially insofar as the family, being a relatively simplified and more psychologically accessible structure to the child, can present the experiences necessary for development so much better than the extant society. Makarenko recognized that the closed communes, such as the Gorki and Dzerzhinski colonies, could very easily provide these experiences. The youths failed, however, to make an easy transition to the outside world, and Makarenko, for reasons of practical politics if nothing else, pointed out that despite the success of the Dzerzhinski Commune "it is better to provide such brakes [on individualism] in the family itself" (p. 131).

THE FORM OF THE FAMILY

Because Makarenko saw society as a monistic whole, and the family as an organic part of that whole, he was prone to think that the family should repeat the total social structure rather than assume one of its own. That is, Makarenko wanted all subdivisions of society to be isomorphous with the whole. Thus, the Rabfak, the farm collectives, the school, the colonies, the family—all forms of social grouping—should be organized in miniature upon the master model of the total society. The primary character of the family was its collectivity, and therefore it had to have sufficient numbers to assume this character. One of the chief reasons for the antisocial nature of the bourgeois family, Makarenko felt, was the fact that it failed, often through simple lack of numbers, to develop a true collective spirit. Conversely, the lack of numbers would assist the development of the bourgeois spirit. Therefore Makarenko was especially insistent that the family had to consist of more than one child. This he pointed out clearly in numerous instances, typlified by the following:

> The danger of bringing up an only child in a Soviet family really amounts to the fact that the family loses the qualities of a collective body. Under the "only-child" system, loss of collectivity comes about as a matter of course: the family simply does not possess enough physical elements to make up a collective; both in quantity and variety of type, father, mother, and son are likely to form such a slender structure that it collapses at the first sign of disproportion, and such disproportion always arises out of the central position of the child (p. 131).

Again, Makarenko emphasized in another passage the specifically educational function that the family serves, and the fact that an educational function cannot be discharged properly unless the family has the true collective character. Thus he wrote,

A Soviet family should never be anything but a collective body. In losing its character as a collective, the family loses much of its significance as an organization of education and happiness. There are various ways of losing the character of a collective. One of the most widespread is the so-called "only-child system" (p. 115).

The substantiation of such a position is difficult to present by experimental or scientific methods. Makarenko never attempted to do so. On the one hand, he had statistical evidence to guide him, illustrating an increase in divorce and marital instability among marriages with none or few children; but more importantly he relied on his own observations and considerably wide experiences, giving to this the added weight of his own ability to construct the position theoretically as he saw that it ought to be. In this respect, the fact is probably of some importance that Makarenko was himself childless and had married late in life, well after his educational views had been established. Indeed, the sole personal influence that could possibly have acted on him was his aged mother who came to live out the last years of her life in the Gorki Colony and was known affectionately by the colonists as "Granny." The extent of this influence, however, must be tempered by Makarenko's view of her as one "whose life was quietly flowing into the final reaches of eventide, veiled by calm, transparent clouds." [2]

In considering the problem of home upbringing, Makarenko was concerned to make certain normative judgments and to develop his thoughts according to them. There is never any hint that Makarenko saw the family as a different and unique social institution cultivating qualities unlike those that came from the rest of the social round. Nor did Makarenko attempt to study the form of the family in an effort to find any rationalization of its current function. Had he done that, of course, he would have perhaps come up against evidence that would oppose his position. Indeed, what he saw of the one-child family definitely convinced him that its current form was not at all felicitous, but instead was misdeveloped and unnatural. His views on this matter are quite pronounced. Thus he wrote that

> In the bourgeois family the only child does not present such a social danger as in ours, because the very character of society does not contradict the qualities cultivated in single offspring. Cold harshness of character, covered by a formal politeness, weak emotions of sympathy, the habit of individual egoism, deliberate careerism and moral evasiveness, indifference to humanity as a whole—all this is natural in a bourgeois society, while it is pathological and harmful in Soviet society (p. 130).

The use of the word "natural" in a bourgeois society needs closer examination. Makarenko uses the word "yestestvenno" for natural, which has in Russian the same vagueness and lack of precision that its counterpart in English has. It can mean both natural in the sense of biologically given but also in the sense of being habitual or customary, although generally its emphasis is devoted to the latter usage. Makarenko is given to the free use of the word "nature," and when he is concerned to emphasize the biologically-given characteristics, he uses the word "priroda" (nature), often using it in the form "priroda-mat" (mother nature). When he speaks of man being under the laws of nature, he is referring to "priroda" (zakon prirod'i).

The confusion between the two usages, and the shift from one to the other, is as marked in English as it is in Russian; certainly the issue is by no means settled. Just precisely what is due to biologically-given nature and what depends upon customs so habituated that they are natural within the total memory of the race is a point of considerable dispute. But there is no doubt that, at least in terms of practice, educators are coming around to the belief given clearly by Ortega y Gasset that "man has no nature, only history." [3] That is, the only nature that man has is the consciousness of himself as part of a continuing cultural process. Makarenko would agree with such a belief, but not for the same reasons. Ortega was concerned to present an idealistic version of human nature while Makarenko wanted to give an environmentalist and behaviorist version; Makarenko's aim was to emphasize the complete dominance of conditioning upon human behavior. In this way, he was able to shift quite freely from one connotation of the term "nature" to the other without any apparent ambiguity or confusion. Nature, for him, was precisely what was natural to man, natural being that which could be performed without any particular violence being done to the personality. Thus, if a particular habit could be cultivated without causing strain in a person, Makarenko would regard it as being in accord with the person's nature, and hence "natural." In this way he could show that greed and callousness was natural in the bourgeois man, and altruism and social concern to be natural in the Soviet man. His implicit faith in the power of environmental conditioning to produce the desired qualities was striking. He reported that

I profess infinite, reckless and unhesitating belief in the unlimited power of educational work, particularly under the social conditions pertaining in the Soviet Union. I do not know a single case where a genuinely valuable character was formed without a healthy educational background or, on the contrary, where a perverted character came about in spite of correct educational work (p. 77).

From the point of view of the family, a healthy educational background meant a home in which there were other children, Makarenko's support coming from the to him obvious evidence. Thus he argued that

Millions of examples—yes, millions—can be brought forward to confirm the huge successes of children from big families. And, on the contrary, the successes of only children are extremely rare. As far as I have been concerned personally, my encounters with the most unbridled egoism, which destroys not only parental happiness but also the successes of the children themselves, have almost always been with only sons and daughters (p. 130).

In this regard it is only fair to point out that after the original flood of besprizorniki had been settled, Makarenko was dealing with true delinquents in the Western sense of the word, and a considerable proportion of these, whose lives he was intimately acquainted with in the colonies, came from homes in which there were no other children. At the same time, another word of caution is apposite. Makarenko's concern, as shown in *A Book for Parents,* was to a large extent occupied with certain superficial features of family life—a preoccupation with things like its size and physical make-up. Being opposed to psychological analysis, he made no attempt to analyze the family more deeply. Thus he was unable to declare precisely what it was within the large family that produced qualities that he admired. He never concerned himself, that is, with the deeper psychological structure of the family. Had he done so, he would of course have found that even within large families there are those who live lives of "only children." Within many large families there are children who become withdrawn and fail to be completely absorbed into the collective spirit, just as Grisha Ryzhikov lived within, but apart from, the Dzerzhinski Commune. Conversely, many "only" children are not disproportionately developed, but can exhibit all of the qualities of other children from larger families.

Makarenko's failure to examine the psychological structure of the family was not due to his ignorance. On the contrary, he was conscious of the methods but distrusted the results. For Makarenko, psychological analysis would yield no positive program for the future. In his view, psychology was essentially backward-looking insofar as it sought answers to what had passed. His concern was with the future and, having pinned his hopes to the power of environmental conditioning, he was not intent on finding psychological evidence to refute it. In his speech given in Leningrad in 1938, five months before his death, he stated his views quite emphatically. Questioned on his refusal to accept the invitation to contribute to a Soviet text on pedagogy, he gave the following answer:

I was invited by the professors to help with this book. I agreed on the one condition that they would tell me whether we should be writing about the pedagogics of today or the future. They said that it was not possible to write about the pedagogical science of the future. So I answered them that if we are to write about the pedagogics of today, life will overtake us and the result will be that we shall have written about yesterday's methods.[4]

Instead of concerning himself with such a method, Makarenko turned his attention to the pedagogics of the future and directed attention in his study of the family to its organization. That is, in his quest for the reconstruction of Soviet society he sought to give the family such an organization as to make it capable of achieving the production of the new citizen through its methods of organization.

THE ORGANIZATION OF THE FAMILY

In line with his general views on the nature of the family, Makarenko saw that it must repeat the total Soviet society in every possible way. Hence, in seeking complete isomorphism, he patterned the organization and authority of the family on that of the wider society. He took it as self-evident, of course, that wholeness and unity in the family collective are fundamental qualities. The Five Year plans, the success of the New Economic Policy, and the collectivization of agriculture meant that the economic basis of the family, common to all primitive and agrarian cultures, was removed. Henceforth, the family existed upon fewer bases and, with the removal of the economic basis, he argued that "our family is no longer an isolated group of paternal possessions" (p. 36).

Nevertheless, Makarenko did not imply that the family was a purely political form of organization. On the contrary, he stated that the family is not a chance combination of members of society. The family is a natural [yestestvennyi] collective body and, like everything natural [yestestvennoe], healthy and normal, it can only blossom forth in socialist society, freed of those very curses from which both mankind as a whole and the individual are indeed freeing themselves.

The family becomes the natural [yestestvennyi] primary cell of society, the place where the delight of human life is realized, where the triumphant forces of man are refreshed, where children—the chief joy of life—live and grow (p. 36).

It is clear from his choice of the word for "natural" (yestestvennyi) that he was not secure in his knowledge of the origin of the normalcy of the family. However, Makarenko did not then continue to postulate that the "natural" basis of the family carried with it a corresponding authority and system of organization that came from "nature." He was emphatic in declaring that both the organization and authority of the family were derived from the higher Soviet society. Thus,

Our parents are not without authority either, but this authority is only the reflection of social authority. The duty of a father in our country towards his children is a particular form of his duty towards society.

...In handing over to you a certain measure of social authority the Soviet state demands from you correct upbringing of future citizens (pp. 36–37).

It was the point that the child is as much a member of the total society as of the family that Makarenko was concerned to emphasize. In peasant Russia, for the preceding centuries, children were, as in many other countries, considerably ill-used, without any rights whatsoever. The rights of the father over his family were almost absolute. On their accession to power, the Bolsheviks passed a series of sweeping social reforms that gave a considerable measure of state protection to children. Thus Article 153 of the *Original Family Law of the Russian Soviet Republic* stated quite emphatically that "Parental rights are exercised exclusively for the benefit of the children." [5] Within the same code, other articles (Articles

145 through 166) determined that parents have the responsibility for providing shelter, food, and an education for their children up to the age of eighteen for boys and sixteen for girls. In addition, they must provide a home life that is conducive to the over-all welfare and happiness of the child. Provisions were also made within the same code for the removal of children from harmful homes and for the treatment of both parents and children according to the directions of the presiding court.

Makarenko's interests went beyond simple humanitarian improvements, desirable as he knew them to be. For Makarenko, the home and family was the place where collectivity and morality, in the new Communist pattern, were to be taught. If the family were to be allowed to retain its absolute character, then it could impede the development of a total social consciousness and the complete dissemination of Soviet sovereignty. The parents, exercising a delegated authority, had the responsibility of assuming command in the family. Parents had to be firm in their control, and they had to make it clear to the children that they were the officers of the greater Soviet society. Thus Makarenko stressed the necessity for the maintenance of formal authority in the home. There is a place for friendship between parent and child, "but the father still remains a father and the son remains a son, that is, a boy who needs to be brought up; and it is the father who brings him up, thus acquiring certain characteristics besides his position of friend" (p. 249). If this is not secured, then Makarenko asserts that "it is difficult to make out who is bringing up whom" (p. 251).

Upon the parents, then, devolved the responsibility for organizing the family so that it provided the child with a model of the wider Soviet society; within the family the responsibilities of a Soviet citizen, as well as the development of a respect for authority, were to be learned. In the properly conducted family, the child is disciplined, not according to careless and random parental responses to various actions,

but in a total, over-all way so that the child is able to comprehend the pattern of Soviet authority. Makarenko eschewed
the use of physical force or violence, pointing out that a
parent commands respect and obedience, first by assuming
the role of leader and then by ordering the family in such a
firm way that the child is made secure and given definite sta-
tus within its structure. But in showing precisely how this is
achieved, Makarenko retreated into the realm of intuition.
It was characteristic of Makarenko that he was a fine judge of
human relations and could tell, intuitively, how far he could
push issues. This was made abundantly clear in his descrip-
tions of life in the youth colonies. In the problem of child
training, he again relied upon his intuition, and pointed out
that the over-all characteristic of the family was its "tone," a
condition in the family corresponding to the life style of the
collective. Other writers have described the same phenomenon under the title of his "sense of the mean." [6]

Authority for children had to be the same authority that
obtained in Soviet society outside the family, and this authority had to be "embodied in the parents themselves, irrespective of their relations to children. . . . Its roots are always
to be found in one place: in the parents' conduct . . ." (p.
179). And this authority shows itself up in the general tone
of the parents' lives. If parents are themselves governed by
the Soviet morality, then their lives will exhibit this general
tone. In making this assertion, Makarenko is getting at a
fundamental truth, and his statement in this regard has a
universal message. Thus he said that

no problems of authority, freedom and discipline in the family
collective can be solved by any artificially devised tricks or
methods. The process of upbringing is a constant process, and
its separate details find their solution in the *general tone* of the
family, and general tone cannot be invented and artificially
maintained. General tone, dear parents, is created by your own
lives and your own conduct. The most correct, reasonable, well
thought-out methods of upbringing will be of no use if the general tone of your life is bad. And, on the contrary, only correct

general tone will suggest to you both correct methods of training a child, and, above all, correct forms of discipline, work, freedom, play and . . . authority (p. 179).

Because he was dealing with one of the most intangible of human relationships, Makarenko presented his views through the didactic story technique of *A Book for Parents*, rather than through a more formal, analytic technique.

THE FAMILY AND MORAL GROWTH

If the family is permeated with this "general tone," and is organized according to the strict pattern of delegated authority, Makarenko argued, then it will be in its most suitable condition for the cultivation of a true Soviet outlook. In developing his notions of the family, Makarenko built onto his ideas of the "form" of the collective. Makarenko thought that the family needed a strong external structure for the same reasons that the colonists needed it: discipline and duty were in essence difficult to render, and the provision of a strong external system helped to assist this. Fundamentally, the task of the family was to ensure the cultivation of the moral person, one who was able to act completely and unhesitatingly in accordance with the requirements of the greater morality of society. This was the primary task of the family as Makarenko saw it, and in this connection he wrote that

Moral depth and unity of family collective experience is a completely necessary condition of Soviet upbringing. This applies equally both to families with enough and to families with less than enough.

In our country he alone is a man of worth whose needs and desires are the needs and desires of a collectivist. Our family offers rich soil for the cultivation of such collectivism (p. 53).

If the family is so arranged, then morality is taught as the standard of everyday life. Makarenko believed that in a truly Soviet household there could be only one standard of morality, and that that had to permeate every waking action and thought. He was derisive of the "Sunday morality" of Western Christendom where "the yardstick of morality was not moral excellence but common everyday sinfulness" (p. 407). The church had contributed especially to this, simply requiring one to "listen for a few hours to the nasal singing of the sexton, duck under the greasy stole of the priest for a minute . . . and 'write off' all one's misdeeds" (p. 407). However, the use of only one standard of morality, based on a complete consciousness and acceptance of collectivity, meant, at least in theory, that many problems would disappear. The perennially thorny problem of sex in the lives of adolescents, Makarenko argued, would fail to achieve the prominence it has in the West because it would be dealt with as a normal aspect of collective living. And because the cultivation of a true Soviet morality, like duty and discipline, would be no easy task, Makarenko urged that the family develop a strong, well-ordered regimen of living. Such a regimen, he insisted, was "most essential training for the will" (p. 302).

THE TOTAL STATE AND A TOTAL MORALITY

There is much in Makarenko's view of the family that seems universal and that has been generally practiced in other societies for considerable periods. Yet there is a feature that makes his view distinctive, if not totally unique. This is his thoroughgoing insistence upon the extension of the morality of family living to all aspects of outside life. The distinctiveness of this can be best illustrated by its limits. The child could, in strict accordance with the theory, denounce his own parents. Authority rested ultimately in the society, and the parents held it only by direct delegation. As developed by Makarenko, of course, such a position would be most repugnant; nonetheless it is a possible extreme to which his system could extend.

The position to which Makarenko was working in his thought was one where the ultimate criteria of truth and morality rested in the total state and permeated downward to the people through the various state agencies, including the family. Originally morality came not from the people but from an idealistic, theoretically-derived premise. Because the people were not anxious to embrace the new ideal, it was essential to develop a consciousness of the need to cultivate those qualities of the will that would ensure the acceptance of the new morality. Makarenko, as educator, saw that this had to begin as soon as possible. Boldyrevas, a Lithuanian Soviet educator, has described the early education of the child through Makarenko's methods in the following words: "Soviet patriotism, proletarian internationalism, a communist view of labor and public property, discipline, collectivism, truthfulness, self-criticism—these are the most important characteristics that the child should acquire." [7]

Whereas Makarenko felt that all failures in upbringing in the bourgeois world could be traced directly to the cultivation of greed, regulated by competition (pp. 404–5), in Soviet society he was certain that the cultivation of a communist morality would lead to the development of wholesome personalities. The socialist state requires a total morality, insofar as "In socialist society the demands of morality apply to everybody, and everybody must respond to them" (p. 407). Therefore, "in socialist society, based upon the reasonable idea of solidarity, the moral action is simultaneously the wisest one (p. 406). The notion of a communist morality must of necessity color all of Soviet life, and therefore education, if the new era is to be gained. Thus Makarenko insisted that the communist morality had to extend into all aspects of life, and could not be a "morality of abstention" (p. 408). It must be a morality pervading life at all levels, and the moral education of the child must proceed from the earliest possible moment. In giving direction to this thought,

he showed his belief that "If extended to make a philosophical generalization, the idea of solidarity embraces all spheres
of life" (p. 408).

Thus, in the closing years of Makarenko's thought, the
family became one of the prime instruments for achieving
the total state; the solidaristic, unified society. Many of his
notions would be warmly applauded in the West, much of
his analysis is sound and is based not on Marxist dogma and
ideology but on shrewd common sense and a broad, genuine
humanitarianism. Few would quibble with his view that
the same standards of moral worth should apply to all actions. Where exception can be taken to his views is with his
notion of the complete merging of the family with the rest
of the social structure, and his failure to indicate how values
could arise from the people themselves and become incorporated in the ideology. For this, Makarenko had no theory.
At the same time, of course, he himself was still but on the
fringe of the problem and did not anticipate *A Book for
Parents* becoming his last word on the matter. Indeed, as he
closed the book, he pointed out that "We cannot yet say that
we have finally mastered the dialectics of communist morality" (p. 408). To be fair, in the closing paragraph Makarenko
announced his intention of examining "the problems of the
spiritual and material culture of the family, and of aesthetic
education" (p. 410), and to that end he invited his readers to
write of their experiences to him. Had he been able to do
so, it could be that Makarenko would have developed his
theory to the point where a more thoroughgoing criticism
could be made.

CHAPTER 12
MAKARENKO'S CONTRIBUTION
TO EDUCATION

THE IMPORTANCE OF MAKARENKO'S
EDUCATIONAL THOUGHT

In assessing Makarenko's contribution to educational thought, there are two issues that have to be separated. One is his contribution to educational thought and practice in terms of its applicability to the Russian social system; the other, and for us in the West an equally important issue, is the wider applicability of his thought and practice to the whole social order. Within Russia it seems that Makarenko's work has made its mark. The pre-eminence accorded his name and the emphasis given to his writings are testimony to the success of his ideas. Lilge, as a result of a recent visit to Russia, reported that the majority of educators to whom he spoke consciously accepted Makarenko in some form or other as their educational model and mentor.[1] Similarly, Lawrence has offered the argument that "the principles which were worked out in the colonies were of much wider application and were felt by Makarenko and increasingly by others to be basic for Soviet education." [2]

Apart from the intrinsic interest given by his work, there are two fundamental issues to be explored in relation to Makarenko's work that have a bearing upon education in the

West. Is Makarenko's system a total educational system? And is his system applicable to society outside the totalitarian state?

The first of these issues raises the possibility that Makarenko's work is really confined only to the realm of educational psychology, even if it is, as Lawrence argues, difficult and challenging, and totally unlike conventional progressive child psychology.[3] That is, the values and social norms that are incorporated within the personality are themselves not derived from the educational process but are taken from the extant social order. If this is so, then Makarenko's system of itself is not sufficient for the production of the new society, but is simply instrumental for attaining purposes derived from outside the educational process. Indeed, in many of its features the system developed by Makarenko is similar to that of John Dewey, and this raises a host of interesting speculations. Both, for example, saw education fundamentally as a group process, with discipline a group function; both saw the teacher as a more mature person, charged with the task of simplifying the external social order and of presenting and manipulating it in order that the young will be able to take on the values and morals of the wider society; both saw great value and dignity in work and argued that labor, along with all forms of creative endeavor, was of the highest educational value, producing the completely cultured, roundly-developed person. Yet Dewey always saw values arising within the educative process, and for him education was its own end.

Although Dewey believed in a unitary, monistic society, he saw that the whole must be necessarily divided into parts with varying functions. In this respect Dewey recognized the need for special as well as for general education. Special education he saw in close relation to vocational education, both being the outcomes of particular individual interests. Society, for Dewey, was strengthened by the variety of diverse skills, interests, and talents that its individual members brought to it. Far from denying individual interests, Dewey saw them as necessary for the continued enrichment of the culture—as essential, in a phrase, to social growth. Makarenko, for his part, never made such a distinction; at this point emerges one of the fundamental differences between Makarenko's system and a popular Western system such as Dewey's.

In Makarenko's theory, the demands made by the group or by society are prior. In its forward progression, society develops needs for skills and competences. By some process that is obscure in Makarenko's thinking, the group needs are transmitted to the members of the group, who in turn take on themselves the responsibility of meeting these needs. Interest, when it is present, is subordinated to the overwhelming needs of collective life. Indeed, in Makarenko's system, interest is not required at all. Its place is taken by the twin virtues of duty and discipline. Makarenko was always strong in his denunciation of interest that was merely "self-interest." Even when the individual performed altruistic, selfless acts in the group interest they were condemned if they came as the result of individual initiative. This is well illustrated in the actions of Lyonya during a village flood. When the river overflowed its banks, the nearby factory workers were organized into flood-relief parties according to their factory shifts. Lyonya, when his shift was over, refused to cease digging the levees. This brought upon him considerable vituperation from his workmates, the final sting being given by Minayev. After stating, "And you've no discipline," Minayev goes on to say "We don't need your heroism at the moment. There are plenty of heroes like you here. But you seem to want to show off, as if you were better than anyone else." [4]

This issue brings out a dilemma that Makarenko was never able to resolve satisfactorily: the conflict between censure of individual overperformance and the encouragement of Stakhanovism. Makarenko failed to elaborate a theory of the manner in which individuals follow interests and of the way in which particular vocational specialties are chosen and followed. It seems that children were allowed, in practice, to follow their own interests when this was in the interests of the group, although the children were never encouraged to recognize any element of conscious choice. On the contrary, they were led to believe that they had acted in accordance with the wider needs of the collective. At times, children were actively prevented from following their own lines of interest when they conflicted with group needs. This means that the individual is required to act in accordance with group demands, while at the same time striving to meet these demands as fully as possible. A balance between subordination of the self on the one hand and voluntary overproduction on the other is required of each person.

To secure individual subordination, Makarenko elaborated his theory of discipline and duty. Yet, as even these virtues can fail if the task lacks interest, he was forced to accept such things as external goals, competition, and Stakhanovism in order to meet the needs for production. To a large extent this was compatible with his notion of external challenges producing the necessary motivation for social action. At the same time it does not produce a satisfactory theory of purpose behind human endeavor; his theory gives little attention to the role of deliberate creative action. As such, it fails to elaborate a theory of any distinctively human purposes to life.

This will, inevitably, lead into the second issue, the applicability of Makarenko's system to the outside world. Apart from any practical applicability that Makarenko's system might have beyond the Soviet Union, his theory and educational ideas will have tremendous importance in giving direction to our own thought, and in supplying answers to questions which we might well ask but which, through the structure of our own society and educational systems, we will be unable to put to the test. The final test of the greatness of any scheme of education rests upon its wider applicability, its capability of being used at other times and other places.

Makarenko drew his educational ideas primarily from his social and philosophical beliefs, giving his educational ideas form and sanction from empirically-derived evidence. Education in his view was not a primary activity, but was derived from and dependent on certain philosophical premises. These premises Makarenko never derived for himself; rather, they were accepted completely from the Hegelian-Marxist system of the Revolution. Further, Makarenko never questioned these beliefs but, to the end of his career, took them as given. Only in the latter pages of *A Book for Parents* (in early editions) did he give voice to some doubts and qualms. In the development of his pedagogy, however, Makarenko held closely all along to the Marxist view of things. If he did deviate from the party line, it was in the direction of giving greater emphasis to the Hegelian rather than to the Marxist aspect.

In essence, society for Makarenko was monist; in addition, it was developing in a forward progression. Makarenko never gave voice to his views on the absolute nature of the universe, and he never directly asserted a materialist view of things. It is true that in all of his writings there is a distinctly anticlerical attitude, but this does not necessarily entail denial of ultimate spiritual values. On the contrary, Makarenko leant heavily on traditional Russian religious intuitivism, and there were instances where he evaded solving problems according to the dictates of the new social order because they failed to provide a satisfactory emotional answer. When Vera, one of the colonists at Kuryazh, became illegitimately pregnant, Makarenko refused to give her the simple permit for a legal abortion which was all that Soviet law demanded. Instead, he forced her to continue her pregnancy, feeling somehow that it would be better for her in the long run.[5]

Instead of taking a straightforward materialist view of life, Makarenko asserted that human values were primary despite the official Soviet view that society was developing in a forward dialectic progression. Makarenko saw ultimate values in an increased respect for human dignity, in an ever greater assertion of the values of human life. The economic liberation of man, and the achievement of the state ownership of the means of production, in his view were but secondary and provided only the means to the ultimate liberation and enrichment of each person's life. He never doubted the necessity for economic serfdom to disappear before man could be culturally free; but his vision was always directed toward this cultural liberation itself. This liberation meant, of course, not a reassertion of individual rights but the removal of the pathology of separate lives and the complete, ultimate union of the individual and the society. Makarenko's vision was of an ideal, logical order, existing in the ultimately realizable future, a vision seen through his "system of perspectives."

The attainment of the ideal, logical order was the task of education. In believing that the new, logical, ideal order was realizable, however distantly, Makarenko developed a belief in the need to re-educate individuals to take their places in such a social order. Such individuals would have to be completely consonant with the new order. In a sense, they would have to be created in its image. At the same time, however, Makarenko was not completely secure in his vision. Given only in broad generalizations, its details were as yet unlimned and the methods and procedures by which both the new society and the new man could be produced were unknown. To this extent his practice did affect the nature of his philosophical views. Education was the task of developing and expanding the individual psychological order to the point where it fitted coincidently with the total, social, ideal, logical order.

To achieve this expansion of the individual to the point where there was complete harmony with the outside social order, Makarenko moved in two directions. In his practice, he sought to educate the child according to an environmentalist psychology where social conditioning and habituation took a prominent place. Theoretically, he sought to develop a notion of the society as a completely educative society, where all of its parts and functions were devoted to the single overmastering task of the production of the complete citizen. To this end, the school, the factory, the collective farm, the family—all social groupings—were considered to be primarily educative, and to be psychologically structured so as to better afford the training of the individual in group ways. Society, in Makarenko's vision of things, was a grand ordering of units, each isomorphous with the whole, each demanding complete loyalty and self-discipline, and yet at the same time able to be absorbed completely into the wider scheme. No unit was to achieve isolation or differentiation of psychological function from the rest of the units. Thus for Makarenko the terms "education" and "socialization" were synonymous.

Nevertheless, Makarenko was realistic in his views, and he knew that the two chief influences on the child, especially in the early formative years, were the home and the school. After the failure of the new order to eliminate the family, Makarenko revised his strategy to account for the value of the family in socialist terms and was able to devise an educative function for it. Thus, in considering Makarenko as an educator, it is primarily his work in the school and his views on the home and family life that recommend him. The difference between these two institutions was not so much in function as in the period of the day for which it had responsibility for the child. While in practice the home might have to assume certain special responsibilities, such as the provision of food, shelter, and affection, along with training in practices like hygiene, and while the school might have responsibility for transmitting certain intellectual learnings, yet this was not the primary distinction, a view which to Western educators is most unusual. The division was simply in terms of time. The home was recognized, however, as a place where such individual, intensified education could be carried on as the school would be unable to handle.

Despite Makarenko's apparently clear vision of the purpose of education, the nature of the educative process was almost as unknown to him as it was to the rest of the Soviet educators. The acceptance of such broad, visionary postulates and their implementation were considerable tasks. It is one of Makarenko's successes and one of his contributions to educational theory that he undertook to construct a suitable educational process and, relative to his purposes, was more than successful in so doing. In achieving this, he moved beyond narrow and local success in educational endeavor and made his name secure in the history of education. Standing out as Makarenko's signal achievement is his construction of a theory and practice of education designed to implement the ideal state. It is important not to discredit the man's work simply because he moved in a social and ideological milieu different from our own. It is to Makarenko's credit that he sought more energetically and more devotedly than most of us to make the world a better place in which to live. In the West we are not anxious to accept all of his work, chiefly because we reject certain of his views on society and the origin of morality, but nonetheless it should not prevent us from appreciating the greatness of his contribution. Further, much of his work is of value in helping us to appreciate the difficulties in the way of implementing the millennium; it can guide our thinking about the necessary safeguards that have to be maintained in our own social system.

THE NATURE OF THE EDUCATIVE PROCESS

As the preceding section showed, the aims of education, for Makarenko, were to bring the individual to the point where his views, ideals, beliefs, desires, and actions were in complete harmony with those of the wider group. That is, education was the means whereby the individual, psychological view of the world was expanded, developed, and restructured so that it became coincident with the logical, ideal society toward which Makarenko divined that Russia was going. Believing in a group that transcended the lives of the individuals composing it, he saw education as the process of helping each person to achieve total "groupness" of mind and action. In developing an educational method to achieve this, Makarenko made his great contribution.

The ideal state was viewed by Makarenko in terms of current desires; that is, he saw it as an industrial, highly mechanized state with high productivity and a favorable economic outlook. To achieve this, the total education of every person was required. The monistic view of society prevented the development of people with marked specialties—indeed, specialties led to division of the body social, and to pathologies of the social structure. The education of the new citizen had to be concerned with all-round growth in an industrial society—that is, polytechnical education. Believing that a cultured man in a technical society needs to be familiar with the technology itself, Makarenko set to implement this with a will. By having each person go through certain of the processes and techniques of the industrial society, an appreciation of the whole society and of its necessary interrelatedness could be had. Thus, in his communes, Makarenko divided the school day into two halves—one half in the classroom learning formal materials, and the other half in the shops where the children worked at assembly lines making furniture, electric drills and thirty-five millimeter cameras for sale to the outside society, in addition to making their own clothing and meeting much of their domestic requirements.

The content of the curriculum, consequently, was arranged to afford each child the maximum contact with the fundamental activities of an industrial society; in so doing, two great purposes would be worked toward: all-round growth in an industrial culture and the cultivation of a solidaristic society through appropriate activities. Makarenko believed that it was essential to provide conjoint working activities if men were to develop a truly socialist consciousness. By participation in shared activities he believed that they would develop an appreciation and a willingness to enter into the communist mode of life (which, it is important to remember, he considered the highest and truest form of human existence).

This sort of notion of conjoined activities, which has enjoyed considerable currency in various forms over the years in Western society, had been developed in Makarenko's time by Lenin. It became an important tenet in the general social reconstruction doctrine of the Leninist period, and before that in Marxism generally. At this point it seems most likely that Makarenko was echoing the sentiments of his masters. But the cry was not universally taken up in the new Soviet society, the reality of the total political and economic situation being such that polytechnization was a sort of socialist luxury at the time. The cry has been renewed from time to time, the most recent issue coming from Nikita Khrushchev, who, in an address to the full assembly of the Central Committee of the Communist Party in 1958, gave the fundamental Leninist position. Thus he reasserted the doctrine that "the harmonious development of man is unthinkable without physical labor which is creative and joyous, which strengthens the organism and heightens its vital functions." [6]

In Khrushchev's speech these sentiments are normative rather than descriptive, and were intended as a basis from which a program of future educational practice in the USSR could be developed. That his words were not descriptive is obvious from the nature and purpose of the address itself. The current facts of Soviet society are that basic divisions have appeared as the state has become increasingly in need of people to discharge intellectual functions. To combat the

growing sense of identity that this group has been developing and their consequent influence, which could conceivably
constitute a threat to the regime, the Communist Party, with
Khrushchev as spokesman, moved with this resolution to bring
all children in the Soviet schools "closer to life." Accordingly,
the intention was to ensure that all children were disciplined
in manual labor, explicitly for their more harmonious development, but implicitly in an attempt to neutralize the
growing intellectual caste of mind that some children were
displaying. The difficulties in the way of implementing such
a decision could be considerable, and the fact that Khrushchev's statement remains almost wholly at the normative
level is attested by one observer who, returning from Russia
two years after the proclamation and having seen the educational system in operation prior to 1958, reported that the
old split continues, relatively unchanged.[7]

Makarenko had no particular theory of human nature. As
the preceding chapter pointed out, he used the two words
"yestestvenno" and "priroda" interchangeably and with little ill-effect since he believed in the primacy of conditioning
and environmental training. Yet, in line with his profound
sense of reality, Makarenko knew that whatever human nature is, it responds best when faced with a definite challenge
and set of obligations. The educational process, which Makarenko completely identified with living itself, best proceeded
in a structured situation, one which he defined as the "collective." Education was a process by which groups were subjected to external form and then, having accepted the form,
moved forward to the stage where they would eventually be
autonomous and self-regulating.

The soundness of Makarenko's view of the educational
process depends on the secure conviction that the social
group is indeed the fundamental unit by which people advance their purposes and on a precise knowledge of the manner in which groups are organized and the manner in which
they function. Makarenko, to his own satisfaction, felt that

he had the assurance of this knowledge. From his experiences of over fifteen years in the colonies, he concluded that the social group, strongly organized, was indeed the true vehicle, and that given the conditions of continued challenges that could be met successfully, the social cement necessary for the maintenance of the collective could be assured. To this end, of course, Makarenko was compelled to minimize individual differences and to concentrate on the achievement of solidarity and collectivity.

Fundamental to his system were the concepts of duty and discipline, concepts which earlier had been inimical to the purposes of Soviet educators. It had been the general criticism of Makarenko's beliefs in these ideas, with Chaikin the leading spokesman, which had caused Makarenko to leave the Gorki Colony. In an earlier, more visionary, period, the Soviet theorists had been hoping for the uncoerced resolution of wills, but Makarenko saw that each person had to have the concepts of duty and discipline consciously developed. He distrusted the spontaneous emergence of a collective disposition. Duty and discipline for Makarenko were qualities cultivated within the strong framework of the collective, but which, in time, were completely internalized so that they could be voluntarily exercised. In effect, duty and self-discipline were the criteria of the success of the collective system; their appearance signaled the success of the method.

Beneath the concept of discipline lay that of regime. Insofar as Makarenko argued that discipline was an end product, he found it necessary to rationalize the means whereby such a product could be had. The means by which discipline could be progressively developed is through the maintenance of a strict regime in the lives of children. By 1938, having clearly enunciated this view, Makarenko was able to assert that discipline "is not the means of education, but the result of education." And in his view it is regime that provides the means for shaping the child to the desired end.[8]

In this respect, Makarenko's position stood in direct opposition to the progressive educational theory that was emerging in the United States at the same time. The prevailing view there, first clearly given in Dewey's *Democracy and Education* as early as 1916, was that discipline underlay the whole of the learning process, being in fact a function of the engagement of the learner with the task. So, in the United States, under the influence of Dewey, discipline in education came to be conceived as the increasing ability of the learner to carry tasks through to a satisfactory completion in which the learner had a high degree of involvement, while in Makarenko's theory discipline became the outcome of learning that was dominated by a strong regime without any necessary sense of personal involvement on the part of the learner.

UNIVERSAL VALUES IN MAKARENKO'S
EDUCATIONAL METHODS

In assessing Makarenko's contribution to education, we must return to the original questions. Is his system a thoroughgoing educational system? And is it applicable outside the total state? From the point of view of the Western educator who bases his educational beliefs upon the democratic ethic, the answer must be decidedly in the negative. Although we in the West have much to learn from a study of Makarenko's methods, they will not be applicable in the democratic state without qualification.

Basic to any democratic state, if it is to continue to function in good health, is the fact that it must rest upon a conscious and open acceptance of cultural and social pluralism; nothing short of a complete and thoroughgoing acceptance of diversity and variety can be tolerated. Social regulation, of necessity, must be part of any pluralistic culture; nor is there any necessary antipathy toward social planning, provided that the planning is directed toward the maintenance of the free society. There is danger that planning can become too specific in its intent and so defeat its own purpose; planning for pluralism lays open the possibility that the limit will be passed beyond which the result will be a sham and an artificial product.

Far from lamenting the fact that contemporary cultures are becoming increasingly complex, we should be encouraged by the prospect. The problem for the truly democratic society is one of seeing, not how best to reduce the alternatives that are being presented constantly in all aspects of daily life, but rather how we might best enter into contact with as many of these aspects as possible. The educational job is not one of seeking an irreducible "core" to the culture which must assume an urgent priority and be transmitted to all, irrespective of wishes and interests; rather it becomes a job of attempting to provide the greatest possible number of opportunities for the complexity of pursuits to be entered into and enjoyed. This is the genuinely creative and educative way.

From this viewpoint, Makarenko's system is virtually useless. Not only did it deliberately narrow the possible range of pursuits, it all but eliminated intellectual and noetic enterprise. What bulked large in his system was a narrow range of activities involving behavior of the grosser physical sort, and over these a considerable amount of control could be exercised. But the system conspicuously avoided those activities that would expand the possibilities of independent development. As Makarenko admitted, his system produced no artists.

Certain practical limitations against universality also operated. It seems most doubtful that Makarenko's colonies could have ever gotten very large, for great size in itself invites fragmentation and jealousies. The primary emphasis within the colony was on the monistic subculture of the ingroup projected against the background of a rather diffuse society, a society that the colonists were encouraged to regard as a vague, confused social mass.

Such in-group exclusiveness as Makarenko developed in his colonies is not foreign to our own experience. The success of Father Flanagan's experiment in the United States with a Boys Town, for example, depended in part upon the general antagonism that the idea engendered and the consequent stiffening of the boys' resolve to succeed in spite of opposition. And for the very same reasons, Boys Town is not a generally applicable theory and can work only within a very limited context.[9]

Makarenko in fact appreciated this principle, although he could hardly make it too explicit in his writing. But at heart Makarenko did not want his colonists to blend into the extant society once they left the colony. Instead, he wanted them to display some of the characteristics that he earlier admired in the Soviet police; they were to be supremely self-disciplined, thus being able to provide a model for the emulation of others. In a sense, then, his educational system was not designed specifically for transfer. Rather, because it worked with a special group it seems that it would always have a specific in-group appeal. This in turn works against the possibility of applying such a system of education on a thoroughgoing general basis. In its essence, it depended on the contrast with the rest of society furnished by the lives of the group, although it is even possible that Makarenko was unaware of this fact.

In the final analysis, his educational system fails to satisfy the democratic ethic on three fundamental issues: the source of values, the provisions for criticism, and the means whereby creative growth can be provided and maintained. There is no doubt that, relative to the goals of the Soviet system, Makarenko was eminently successful, and that his educational system was more than just a psychology. It articulated a definite educational form of the political ideology, and it elaborated a set of aims, methods, and content appropriate to the attainment of the goals. Any criticism that we in the West can make must of necessity arise from a consideration of its ap-

plicability to our own society. In rejecting Makarenko for
the West, we do so because of the fundamental assumptions
upon which his education was based. Just so could the Soviet
Union reject our educational theories as inadequate.

In essence, Makarenko's system was designed to ensure the
survival of a particular political system, and the system that
he derived was not systematically developed according to its
own inner logic but in the light of its success in meeting political needs. This is not to say that the West has been blame-
less of the same charge; on the contrary, we are often responsible for employing education for the same purpose—to
inculcate particular political doctrines. This ought to provide
us with considerable reason for thought. If we assume that
the democratic social ethic is the highest good for man, then
education, whatever the politics involved, must face three
issues; values, criticism, and creative growth. In the West
we do consciously use education to further the democratic
way of life; and in order to ensure that it is the democratic
way that is being perpetuated, it is important to see that education is able to provide for the training of the young in
critical thinking and creative growth.

Values for Makarenko were derived from above and were
not created directly from the people. While it is true that it
takes an unusual and perceptive person to extract the values
from the culture and articulate them, it is nevertheless important that these values be of the people, and be subjected
to critical tests. This, from our point of view, is a basic failure in Makarenko's theory. Makarenko believed in a strong
external system to which the individual was made to conform
by the best means possible. If the individual conformed willingly, so much the better. Nevertheless, the values were provided from above, and were to be realized by the individual
as life was worked out under the externally imposed form.
The degree of willingness with which the individual accepted the externally imposed values came to be called discipline, while the responsibility to accept them was duty. In

the degree that the values were difficult to accept, greater success in accepting them meant, inevitably, a higher degree of discipline.

The emphasis on discipline meant, in turn, that the development of criticism was not encouraged by Makarenko. In the West, we strive to inculcate a sense of duty and discipline, but it is based on the inherent right of the individual to criticize the requirements. Further, we have attempted to institutionalize criticism so that it has regularized forms, freely available to each individual. It is, in passing, also true that in the West these are at times abused and restricted. Nevertheless, it remains firmly fixed in the democratic ideology that the right of critical thought belongs to each member of the social order. By contrast, criticism under Makarenko's system was not so institutionalized, depending instead upon informal and irregular means. It is true that criticism could be offered before combined councils in the colonies, but such a method could hardly be considered an encouragement. The denial of criticism always leads to simmering discontent and the development of issues to the point where they erupt, often with particular violence. This was as true of Makarenko's colonies as it has continued to be true of the wider Soviet society.

In this regard, it is interesting to note that Makarenko never particularly stressed the value of literacy, nor did he concern himself with the development of intellectual skills and the cultivation of symbolic thought. Whenever there was a conflict between the formal lessons of the classroom and the productive labor of the colony, the classroom lost out. Never were children subjected to great demands to develop symbolic thought, and for this reason he cannot be now a perfect model for Soviet education. On the contrary, this area was left well alone by Makarenko; he busied himself always with the behavioral aspects of education that could be developed through group life. The private individual world of the mind was never deliberately cultivated; when it was, it came purely from collective needs for certain technical competences.

The subordination of the individual in these aspects leads, from a democratic point of view, to a further failure. If symbolic thought is not cultivated, if criticism is denied and values are imposed, then the very growth of the culture seems to be imperiled. It is too soon to make any assessment of the growth of Soviet communism, but it is a curious fact that Makarenko himself once verged on the problem when he wrote that

I must sorrowfully admit that no writers or artists came from the Gorkyites, and this, not because they did not have enough talent, but for other reasons—life and its practical daily problems engulfed them.[10]

This failure of the collective system points up, in a final analysis, one basic error in the system, at least from a democratic point of view. Makarenko put his emphasis upon the efficacy of certain empirically-derived techniques that were successful for their limited purposes, and within a limited period of time. The system was essentially a limited one because it depended upon a set of static values formed by reaction against a definite system. This, of course, is simply the dialectic process. Nevertheless, the dialectic process can only continue successfully if provision is made for variation of response according to the nature of the current challenge. The whole nature of his system was in opposition to the development of individual vision, initiative, adaptability, invention, innovation. By his own testimony, Makarenko showed an unwillingness to accept the decisions of superior officials. Instead he always gave his allegiance to a higher, abstract ideal authority; by a curious twist, he took on many of the characteristics of the priests he was most concerned to discredit. The fact that his charges also looked to him as the highest authority, and his difficulty both in getting transfer of allegiance and in developing a wider concept of sovereignty, also indicate problems in his system.

Even with these criticisms in mind, it is hard to discredit the man's achievements. Considering the history of Russian education and the enormity of the problem, his accomplishments were of the first order. Makarenko's belief in a socialist utopia was based, not on any political notions, but on an evident and genuine humanitarianism. Within the limited sphere of the youth colonies, there is no doubt that he worked wonders. Despite the fact that his system was not in accord with the democratic concept of an educational system, it nonetheless does have certain definite merits for use in specific contexts, provided that the three criteria for democratic growth are met.

When the times in which Makarenko worked are considered, it is clear that there were few alternatives open to him. The very nature of the besprizorniki demanded vigorous measures of control, and in a shattered society Makarenko's were probably as good as could be found. Indeed, it is hard to criticize Makarenko's methods in respect to the immediate situation—if at all. Where criticism can be leveled justly is at his desire to make absolute the system which had only immediate value. The final test of the greatness of Makarenko will depend on evidence of the capacity of his system to grow and develop as the social situation becomes more settled and secure. At this point, however, we have simply to watch for developments, and the future alone will indicate how accurate were his perceptions and how lasting will be his achievements.

REFERENCE MATTER

NOTES

CHAPTER 1

1 *Bol'shaya Sovetskaya Entsiklopediya,* B. A. Vedenski, Glav-nyi Redaktor, Vtoroe Izdanie. Gosudarstvennoe Nauchnoe Izdatel'stvo, 1948, p. 91.

2 Makarenko, A. S., *The Road to Life,* vol. 1. Foreign Languages Publishing House, Moscow, 1955. Introduction by Y. Medinski, p. 16.

3 Winn, R. B., ed. and trans., *Soviet Psychology: A Symposium* (1961).

4 The resolution of the Plenum of the Central Committee of the Communist Party, November 12, 1958, entitled *On Strengthening the Relationship of the School with Life and on the Further Development of the System of Public Education in the Country,* reasserts the theories on the integration of learning and labor that Makarenko had developed. A translation of this resolution, along with an excellent commentary, may be found in George S. Counts, *Khrushchev and the Central Committee Speak on Education* (1959).

5 Goodman, W. L., *A. S. Makarenko, Russian Teacher* (1949); and Lilge, F., *Anton Semyonovitch Makarenko* (1958).

6 *Road to Life,* a film by Nikolai Ekk, author-director. Produced by MEJRABPOMFILM, Moscow, and given world release in 1933 through Soyuzkino.

7 Kostelianets, B., *A. S. Makarenko,* Kritiko-Biograficheskii Ocherk, Gosudarstvennoe Izdatel'stvo Khudozhestvennoi Literatury, Moskva, 1954, p. 4.

8 Kostelianets, p. 5.

9 Makarenko, *Chest'* (*Honor*), in *Sochineniya v Semi Tomakh* (*Collected Works in Seven Volumes*), vol. 6, p. 15.

10 Kostelianets, *A. S. Makarenko,* p. 5.

11 Kostelianets, pp. 6–7.

12 Kostelianets, pp. 7–8.

CHAPTER 2

1   Pares, B., *Russia,* rev. ed. (1949). For a general discussion
    of this issue, chapter 2 is especially pertinent.
2   Leary, D. B., *Education and Autocracy in Russia* (1919), p.
    49. Leary's statistics are that "The peasantry constituted
    some 94.5 per cent, the lower ranks of the urban population
    some 2.5 per cent, the merchants less than 1 per cent, the
    parish clergy some 1 per cent, finally the nobles and officials,
    from 1.25 to 1.5 per cent."
3   Pinkevitch, A. P., *The New Education in the Soviet Repub-
    lic,* George Counts, ed., Nucia Perlmutter, trans. (1929), p. vi.
4   Johnson, W. H. E., *Russia's Educational Heritage* (1950),
    p. 21.
5   An illustration of this situation may be found in the cele-
    brated "Ordinance on the Cooks' Children." On June 18,
    1887, an ordinance was issued, under the tsar's authority,
    attempting to restrict admission to the high school to the
    children of the upper classes. The ordinance reads, in part,
    that attendance at the gymnasium was to be "limited only
    to such children as are in the charge of persons presenting
    sufficient guarantees that the children are properly taken
    care of.... The gymnasium and progymnasium, therefore,
    shall be freed from the attendance of the children of drivers,
    footmen, cooks, laundry-women, small traders and other
    persons similarly situated, whose children, with the ex-
    ception perhaps of the exceptionally gifted ones, should not
    be encouraged to abandon the social environment to which
    they belong." (Given in Ignatiev, P. N., *et al., Russian
    Schools and Universities in the World War,* 1929, p. 31).
    Had this ordinance been enforced, it would have asserted
    the tsar's supremacy. Hence the zemstvos, to avoid tacit
    acquiescence to the tsar, were forced to oppose the ordinance
    and to support the peasants, which they did successfully.
6   Ignatiev, pp. 5 ff.
7   Ignatiev, p. 20.
8   Ignatiev, p. 100.
9   Pares, *Russia,* p. 50.

CHAPTER 3

1 Circular of the People's Commissaire of Education to All Regional Commissioners of Education, Dec. 24, 1917. (The translation used here and in some of the following quotations is that of Max Eastman in a collection of Soviet decrees and documents entitled *Education and Art in Soviet Russia*, the Socialist Publication Society, New York, n.d.)

2 U.S. Commissioner of Education, *Report of the Commissioner of Education*, June 30, 1918, p. 88.

3 This decree is quoted in Hans, N., and Hessen, S., *Educational Policy in Soviet Russia* (1930), p. 17.

4 *Provision for the Organization of Popular Education in the USSR*, Decree of the Workers' and Peasants' Government, Eastman, *Education and Art . . .*, p. 10.

5 U.S. Commissioner of Education, *Report*, 1918, p. 89.

6 Lunacharski, A., *First Report of the People's Commissar of Education*, 1918.

7 People's Commissar Lepeshinski, paper read at the First All-Russian Congress of Teacher-Internationalists, June 2, 1918 (quoted in Eastman, *Education and Art . . .*, p. 15).

8 Lunacharski, *Self-Education of the Workers; The Cultural Task of the Struggling Proletariat* (a short pamphlet), London, n.d.

9 Lunacharski, *Self-Education of the Workers*.

10 Quoted in Hans and Hessen, *Educational Policy . . .*, p. 21.

11 Lunacharski, *Self-Education of the Workers*.

12 *Collection of Laws and Decrees of the Workers' and Peasants' Government*, 1918, nos. 76–77, art. 818. (The translation of Helen Rapp in Schlesinger, R., *The Family in the USSR*, 1949, has been used. This collection of documents is extremely rich in source material of the period.)

13 Schlesinger, *The Family in the USSR* (1949), p. 33.

14 Semashko, N. (People's Commissar of Health of the USSR), *Health Protection in the USSR* (1934), pp. 82–84. Given in Schlesinger, *The Family in the USSR*, p. 44.

15 Lepeshinski, in Eastman, *Education and Art . . .*, pp. 19–20.

16 Lunacharski, "Declaration of the Principles of the Socialist

School," reported in *Narodnoe Prosveshchenie,* No. 10, June 6, 1918.

17   *The Institute for Child Study,* document given in Eastman, *Education and Art . . .* , p. 36.

18   *Education Act of October 16, 1918,* quoted in Hans and Hessen, *Educational Policy . . .* , p. 18.

19   Pares, *Russia,* pp. 66–67.

CHAPTER 4

1   Epshtein, M., "Besprizorniki v SSSR," in *Bol'shaya Sovets-kaya Entsiklopediya,* Glavnyi Redaktor, O. U. Shmidt, Akt-sionernoe Obshchestvo "Sovetskaya Entsiklopediya," Tom Pyatyi, Moskva, 1927, vol. 5, p. 786.

2   King, B., *Russia Goes to School—A Guide to Soviet Education* (1948), p. 149.

3   Detailed in Wilson, L., *The New Schools of New Russia,* Vanguard Studies of Soviet Russia (no place or publishers, but published in the USA about 1928), pp. 100–4.

4   Epshtein, M., in *Bol'shaya Sovetskaya Entsiklopediya* (1927), p. 786.

5   Makarenko, *The Road to Life,* vol. 2, p. 310. The original discussion occurs in *Pedagogicheskaya Poema,* Tom 2, p. 399. In the original Russian, where the word "waif" is given, Makarenko uses the term *besprizornye.* Readers should note that the inflected nature of Russian will constantly change noun endings in different contexts.

6   Leites, N., "Trends in Affectlessness," in Kluckhohn, C., *et al., Personality in Nature, Society and Culture* (1953), pp. 618–32.

7   Makarenko, *The Road to Life,* vol. 1, p. 26.

8   Zalkind, A., "Besprizornost'," in *Bol'shaya Sovetskaya Entsik-lopediya* (1927), vol. 5, pp. 783 ff. Due to the rarity of this encyclopedia, and to the importance of the article, I have given a full exposition of it in this section, borrowing freely without direct quotation in the interests of connected argument.

CHAPTER 5

1   A. S. Makarenko, *Pedagogicheskaya Poema*, in *Sochineniya v Semi Tomakh*, Izdatel'stvo Akademii Pedagogicheskikh Nauk, Moskva, 1957. (This volume, in pages 737 through 746, contains an excellent brief biography of Makarenko with precise dates for all important events. It has not been translated into English, however.)

CHAPTER 6

1   These lectures, along with a considerable amount of Makarenko's later rationalizations of his work, may be found in his *Izbrannye Pedagogicheskie Sochineniya v Chetyrekh Knigakh (Selected Pedagogical Works in Four Volumes)*, Izdatel'stvo Akademii Pedagogicheskikh Nauk, RSFSR, Moskva, 1949. The particular lecture is entitled "Distsiplina, Rezhim, Nakazaniya i Pooshchreniya," Kniga Chetvertaya, pp. 32–57.

2   There is room for a considerable amount of depth analysis of Makarenko's own subconscious desires with respect to the manner in which the form, which had a definite military flavor, became expressed. Earlier it was pointed out that the army exercised some peculiar fascination for him. His own military career was insignificant, and to be medically discharged with poor eyesight is no fit finish for an ardent fighter. It seems too much of a coincidence that Makarenko admired most in Russia the men of the Soviet police (called by him the *Cheka;* see endnote 3, Chapter 8). His eulogy of them is clearly brought out when he wrote, after being employed by them and doubtless as a subsequent rationalization, that, "Among the Cheka people high intellectual standards combined with education and culture had not assumed the outward expression which I had found so hateful among the former Russian intellectuals. . . . The Cheka people are devoted to principle . . . [they have an] all-pervading good humour, terseness of speech, a dislike of ready-made formulae, the inability to lounge on sofas or sprawl over a

table, and, finally, an unlimited capacity for work . . ." (III, 381–83).
3 *Pedagogicheskaya Poema* (1955), p. 216.

CHAPTER 7

1 Sumner, W. G., *Folkways* (1906).

CHAPTER 8

1 See *Learning to Live*, p. 646 ff.
2 A point of view which runs strongly counter to Western views, given, for example, in W. F. Whyte's *Street Corner Society, The Social Structure of an Italian Slum* (1943).
3 It is odd that Makarenko should use the term "Cheka." This was the name given to the original *Extraordinary Commission for Combatting Counterrevolution and Sabotage* created on December 20, 1917. It was abolished by a decree dated February 6, 1922, and replaced by the GPU until the OGPU was established on July 6, 1923. The term "Cheka" was anachronistic at the time that Makarenko was writing, and is probably due either to the fact that the old name lingered, or that "Cheka" is easier on the ear than "Ogpu." See chapter 1, *passim*, of Wolin and Slusser, *The Soviet Secret Police* (1957).

CHAPTER 9

1 Sidney and Beatrice Webb, *Soviet Communism—A New Civilization?* (1936), II, 897.
2 Here I am following the terminology and concepts of Karl Mannheim in *Ideology and Utopia* (1936).
3 Woody, Thomas, *New Minds, New Men?* (1932), p. 49.
4 Shatski, quoted by Woody, p. 48.
5 Pinkevitch, *The New Education in the Soviet Republic*, p. 7.
6 Wilson, L., *The New Schools of New Russia*, pp. 27–28.
7 Nearing, S., *Education in Soviet Russia* (1926), p. 35.
8 Wilson, L., *The New Schools in New Russia*, p. 65.

9   Nearing, *Education in Soviet Russia,* p. 99.
10 The word Komsomol is, like many such Russian proper nouns, formed from the first syllables of the complete title of the group, the Kommunisticheskii Soyuz Molodezhi, literally, the Communist League of Youth.
11 Krupskaya, N. K., speech entitled "International Children's Week," reported in *Pravda,* July 24–30, and collected in *On Education* (1957), pp. 107–8.
12 Krupskaya, N. K., "The Young Pioneer Movement as a Pedagogical Problem" in *Uchitel'skaya Gazeta,* No. 15, April 8, 1927. Collected in *On Education,* p. 118.
13 Nearing, S., *Education in Soviet Russia,* p. 98 (quoted from *Programmes Officiels,* pp. 47–49).
14 Krupskaya, in *On Education,* pp. 118–22.
15 Krupskaya, in *On Education,* pp. 118–22.
16 Nearing, *Education in Soviet Russia,* p. 42.
17 Nearing, p. 46.
18 Decree of the CEC of the RSFSR, April 1929. Reported in *Izvestia.* See also *International Conciliation* for June 1930, No. 261.
19 The word "urok" is simply the Russian word for lesson, and the "lesson" is similar to the Pestalozzian object-lesson or the Herbartian lesson.
20 Samarin, Vladimir, "The Soviet School, 1936–42" in *Soviet Education,* G. L. Kline, ed. (1937), p. 32.
21 Samarin, in *Soviet Education,* p. 32.
22 "On the Pedological Distortion of the System of the Narkomprosov," *Decree of the Central Committee of the Communist Party,* July 4, 1936, *Izvestia,* Vipusk III, p. 5. Irkutski Gosudarstvennoe Pedagogicheski Institut, 1936.
23 King, Beatrice, *Changing Man—The Education System of the USSR* (1937), p. 108.
24 Counts, George, "Education in the USSR," in *The New Republic,* Feb. 13, 1935, pp. 8–11.
25 King, Beatrice, "The New Decrees on Soviet Education," in *British Russian Gazette and Trade Outlook,* January 1933, p. 105.
26 King, "The New Decrees on Soviet Education," p. 107.
27 Stalin, J., *Vopros'i Leninizma (Problems of Leninism),* 11th

ed., p. 490. (This quotation may be found in the English translation, *Problems of Leninism*, Moscow, 1947, p. 523.)

28 Pankratova, A. M., ed., *Istoriya SSSR*, Gosudarstvennoe Uchebno-Pedagogicheskoe Izdatel'stvo Ministerstva Prosveshcheniya RSFSR, Moskva, 1955, Izdanie 14, p. 338.

29 Pankratova, A. M., p. 339. The entire chapter, 18 "Bor'ba za Zavershenie S roitel'stva Sotsializma" ("The Struggle to Complete the Socialist Structure") gives a good account, although extremely unlike our Western views, of the general history of the period and the emergence of the Stakhanov movement.

30 *Pedagogicheskaya Poema*, p. 739.

CHAPTER 10

1 *The Road to Life*, II, 308.
2 Page 9.
3 The reference here is to the omniscient dictator in George Orwell's novel, *1984* (Harcourt Brace, New York, 1949).
4 "Metodika Organizatsii Vospitatel'nogo Protsessa," in *Collected Works in Seven Volumes*, V, 9.
5 Page 9.
6 Page 10 *passim*.
7 Extracts from a speech entitled "Report of a Discussion About Learning to Live at the Kirov Palace of Culture," Leningrad, October 18, 1938. Reported in *Learning to Live*, Appendix, p. 646.

CHAPTER 11

1 "Ya ne asket, no nuzhna dialektika chuvstv." In *Sochineniya v Semi Tomakh*, Tom 4, *Kniga dlya Roditelei*, p. 334.
2 *The Road to Life*, II, 53.
3 Quoted in Cassirer, Ernst, *An Essay on Man* (1956), p. 218.
4 Report of a discussion on *Learning to Live* held in Leningrad, Oct. 18, 1939; recorded in *Learning to Live*, p. 648.
5 *Code of Laws Concerning the Civil Registration of Deaths, Births and Marriages*, October 17, 1918. In Schlesinger, *The Family in the USSR*, pp. 33–42.

6 Cohen, R. S. "On the Marxist Philosophy of Education" in *Modern Philosophies and Education* (1955), p. 208; and Lilge, F., *Anton Semyonovitch Makarenko, passim.*

7 Boldyrevas, N., *Dorinis Vaiku Auklejimas Seimoje (Moral Education of Children in the Family)*, Kaunas, 1957, p. 4, quoted in Remeikis, Thomas, "Theory and Practice of Communist Education," unpublished master's (political science) thesis, University of Illinois, 1958, p. 48.

CHAPTER 12

1 Lilge, F., *Anton Semyonovitch Makarenko*, p. 50.

2 Lawrence, F., "Makarenko—Pioneer of Communist Education," in *The Modern Quarterly*, vol. 8, number 4, Autumn 1953, p. 234.

3 Lawrence, *Modern Quarterly*, p. 234 ff.

4 *A Book for Parents*, p. 397.

5 *The Road to Life*, III, 330 ff.

6 Counts, G. S., *Khrushchev and the Central Committee Speak on Education* (1959), p. 35.

7 Press, B. K., "Mr. K's Educational Reforms—Two Years Later," *California Teachers' Association Journal*, February 1961.

8 Given in Makarenko's essay, "Distsiplina, Rezhim, Nakazaniya i Pooshchreniya" in *Izbrannye Pedagogicheskie Sochineniya v Chetyrekh Knigakh (Selected Pedagogical Works in Four Volumes)*, vol. 4, pp. 33 ff.

9 See Oursler, F. and W., *Father Flanagan of Boys Town* (1959); and Lunetta, V. N., "A Comparative Study: The Gorky Youth Colony and Boys Town," *Educational Theory*, vol. XI, no. 2, April 1961.

10 *The Road to Life*, III, 410.

BIBLIOGRAPHY

Bol'shaya Sovetskaya Entsiklopediya, O. U. Shmidt, Glavnyi Redaktor (*Great Soviet Encyclopedia,* O. U. Shmidt, General Editor), Tom Pyatyi (Bar'ikova–Bessal'ko), Aktsionernoe Obshchestvo "Sovetskaya Entsiklopediya," Moskva, 1927.

Bol'shaya Sovetskaya Entsiklopediya, B. A. Vedenski, Glavnyi Redaktor (*Great Soviet Encyclopedia,* B. A. Vedenski, General Editor), Vtoroe Izdanie, Gosudarstvennoe Nauchnoe Izdatel'stvo, Moskva, 1948.

Cassirer, Ernst, *An Essay on Man,* Doubleday, New York, 1956.

Central Committee of the Communist Party: Decree *On the Pedological Distortion in the System of the Narkomprosov,* July 4, 1936. Reported in Izvestia, Vipusk III, p. 5.

Cohen, R. S., in *Modern Philosophies and Education,* University of Chicago Press, Chicago, 1955.

Counts, George S., "Education in the USSR," in *The New Republic,* vol. LXXXII, no. 1354, February 13, 1935.

Counts, George S., *Khrushchev and the Central Committee Speak on Education,* University of Pittsburgh Press, Pittsburgh, 1959.

Counts, G. S., and Lodge, N. P., *I Want to be Like Stalin* (from the Russian Text on Pedagogy by B. P. Yesipov and N. K. Goncharov), The John Day Company, New York, 1947.

Dewey, John, "Impressions of Soviet Russia," in *The New Republic,* in 6 parts, November–December, 1928.

Eastman, Max, *Education and Art in Soviet Russia In the Light of Official Decrees and Documents,* The Socialist Publication Society, New York, n. d. (*c.* 1919–20).

Eckardt, Hans von, *Russia,* Knopf, New York, 1932.

Goodman, W. L., *A. S. Makarenko, Russian Teacher,* Routledge and Kegan Paul, London, 1949.

Hans, N., and Hessen, S., *Educational Policy in Soviet Russia,* King and Son, London, 1930.

Ignatiev, P. N., Odinetz, D. M., Novgorotsev, P. J., *Russian Schools and Universities in the World War,* Yale University Press, New Haven, 1929.

International Conciliation (Carnegie Endowment for International Peace), New York, various issues.

Johnson, W. H. E., *Russia's Educational Heritage*, Carnegie Press, Carnegie Institute of Technology, Pittsburgh, 1950.

Kalinin, M. I., *On Communist Education: Selected Speeches and Articles*, Foreign Languages Publishing House, Moscow, 1953.

King, Beatrice, *Changing Man—The Education System of the USSR*, The Viking Press, New York, 1937.

King, Beatrice, *Russia Goes to School—A Guide to Soviet Education*, New Education Book Club, London, 1948.

King, Beatrice, "The New Decrees on Soviet Education," in *British Russian Gazette and Trade Outlook*, January, 1933.

Kline, G. L., ed., *Soviet Education*, Columbia University Press, New York, 1957.

Kluckhohn, C., Murray, H. A., and Schneider, D. M., *Personality in Nature, Society and Culture*, 2nd ed., Cape, London, 1953.

Korolev, F. F., *Ocherki Po Istorii Sovetskoi Shkoly i Pedagogiki (An Outline of the History of Soviet Schools and Pedagogy)*, Izdatel'stvo Akademii Pedagogicheskikh Nauk, RSFSR, Moskva, 1958.

Kostelianets, B., *A. S. Makarenko—Kritiko–Biograficheskii Ocherk (A. S. Makarenko—A Critical Biographical Study)*, Gosudarstvennoe Izdatel'stvo Khudozhestvennoi Literatury, Moskva, 1954.

Krupskaya, N. K., *Izbrannye Pedagogicheskie Proizvedeniya (Selected Writings on Pedagogy)*, Izdatel'stvo Akademii Pedagogicheskikh Nauk, RSFSR, Moskva, 1955.

Krupskaya, N. K., *On Education (Stati i Rechi o Vospitanii)*, G. P. Ivanov–Mumjiev, trans., Foreign Languages Publishing House, Moscow, 1957.

Lawrence, Francis, "Makarenko: Pioneer of Communist Education," in *Modern Quarterly*, vol. 8 (Autumn 1953), pp. 234–40.

Leary, Daniel B., *Education and Autocracy in Russia—From the Origins to the Bolsheviki*, University of Buffalo Press, Buffalo, New York, 1919.

Lilge, F., *Anton Semyonovitch Makarenko*, University of California Press, Berkeley and Los Angeles, 1958.

Lunacharski, A., "Declaration of the Principles of the Socialist School," in *Narodnoe Prosveshchenie*, no. 10, June 6, 1918.

Lunacharski, A., *First Report of the Peoples' Commissar of Education*, 1918.

Lunacharski, A. (People's Commissar for Education under the RSFSR), *Self-Education of the Workers; The Cultural Talk of the Struggling Proletariat*, Workers' Socialist Federation, London, n.d. (*c.* 1918–19).

Lunetta, V. N., "A Comparative Study: The Gorky Youth Colony and Boys Town," *Educational Theory*, vol. XI, no. 2, April 1961.

Makarenko, A. S., *A Book for Parents* (*Kniga dlya Roditelei*), Foreign Languages Publishing House, Moscow, 1954.

Makarenko, A. S., *Learning to Live* (*Flagi na Bashnyakh*), Foreign Languages Publishing House, Moscow, 1953.

Makarenko, A. S., *O Literature* (*On Literature*), Sovetskii Pisatel', Moskva, 1958.

Makarenko, A. S., *Pedagogicheskaya Poema* (*An Epic of Education*), Sovetskii Pisatel', Moskva, 1955.

Makarenko, A. S., *Izbrannye Pedagogicheskie Sochineniya v Chetyrekh Knigakh* (*Selected Pedagogical Works in Four Volumes*), Izdatel'stvo Akademii Pedagogicheskikh Nauk, RSFSR, Moskva, 1949.

Makarenko, A. S., *Sochineniya v Semi Tomakh* (*Collected Works in Seven Volumes*), Izdatel'stvo Akademii Pedagogicheskikh Nauk, RSFSR, Moskva, 1957.

    Tom 1   *Pedagogicheskaya Poema* (*Epic of Education*)

    Tom 2   *Marsh 30 Goda* (*The March of the Year Thirty*)
              FD-1
              Mazhor (*The Major*)

    Tom 3   *Flagi na Bashnyakh* (*Flags on the Battlements, or Learning to Live*)

    Tom 4   *Kniga dlya Roditelei* (*A Book for Parents*)
              Lektsii o Vospitanii Detei (*Lectures on the Education of Children*)
              Vystupleniya po Voprosam Semeinogo Vospitaniya (*Speeches on the Problems of Education in the Family*)

    Tom 5   *Obshchie Voprosy Teorii Pedagogiki* (*General Problems of Pedagogical Theory*)
              Vospitanie v Sovetskoi Shkole (*Education in the Soviet School*)

Tom 6   Chest' (Honor)
Nastoyashchii Kharakter (The Present Character)
Komandirovka (The Mission)
Polemicheskie Stat'i (Polemical Articles)
Tom 7   Publitsistika (Publicism)
Rasskazy i Ocherki (Stories and Sketches)
Stat'i o Literature i Retsenzii (Articles on Litera-
ture and Reviews)
Perepiska c A.M. Gorkim (Correspondence with
Gorki)
Makarenko, A. S., *The Road to Life, An Epic of Education*
(*Putevka v Zhizn', Pedagogicheskaya Poema*), 3 vols., Ivy and
Tatiana Litvinov, trans., Foreign Languages Publishing House,
Moscow, 1955.
Makarenko, A. S., *The Road to Life,* Stephen Garry, trans., vol. 1,
Stanley Nott, London, 1936.
Mannheim, Karl, *Ideology and Utopia,* International Library
of Sociology and Social Reconstruction, London, 1936.
Mead, Margaret *Soviet Attitudes Towards Authority,* McGraw-
Hill, New York, 1951.
Mehnert, K., *Youth in Soviet Russia,* Michael Davidson, trans.,
Harcourt Brace, New York, 1933.
Muller, V. K., ed., *Anglo-Russkii Slovar' (English-Russian Dic-
tionary)*, Gosudarstvennoe Izdatel'stvo Inostrannykh i Na-
tsional'nykh Slovari, Moskva, 1953.
Nearing, Scott, *Education in Soviet Russia,* International Pub-
lishers, New York, 1926.
N.S.S.E., Fifty-fourth Year Book of the National Society for the
Study of Education, Nelson B. Henry, ed., *Modern Philoso-
phies and Education,* University of Chicago Press, Chicago,
1955.
Oursler, F. and W., *Father Flanagan of Boys Town,* Doubleday,
New York, 1959.
Pankratova, A. M., ed., *Istoriya SSSR (A History of the USSR)*,
3 vols., Institut Istorii Academii Nauk SSSR, Gosudarstvennoe
Uchebno-Pedagogicheskoe Izdatel'stvo Ministerstva Prosve-
shcheniya RSFSR, Moskva, 1955.
Pares, Bernard, *Russia,* rev. ed., Mentor, New York, 1949.
Pinkevitch, A. P., *The New Education in the Soviet Republic,*

George Counts, ed., Nucia Perlmutter, trans., The John Day Company, New York, 1929.

Press, B. K., "Mr. K's Educational Reforms—Two Years Later," *California Teachers' Association Journal,* February 1961.

Remeikis, Thomas, "Theory and Practice of Communist Education," unpublished master's (political science) thesis, University of Illinois, Urbana, Illinois, 1958.

Schlesinger, Rudolf, *The Family in the USSR: Documents and Readings,* Rapp, H., trans., Routledge and Kegan Paul, London, 1949.

Schlesinger, Rudolf, *The Nationalities Problem and Soviet Administration, Selected Readings,* W. W. Gottlieb, trans., Routledge and Kegan Paul, London, 1956.

Shore, M. J., *Soviet Education—Its Psychology and Philosophy,* The Philosophical Library, New York, 1947.

Simmons, E. J., *USSR,* Cornell University Press, Ithaca, New York, 1947.

Smirnitski, A. I., ed., *Russko-Angliiskii Slovar'* (*Russian-English Dictionary*), Gosudarstvennoe Izdatel'stvo Inostrann'ikh i Natsional'n'ikh Slovarei, Moskva, 1958.

Stalin, Joseph, *Voprosy Leninizma* (*Problems of Leninism*), Izd. 11, Str 490, Gosudarstvennoe Izdatel'stvo Nauk, RSFSR, Moskva, 1947.

Sumner, W. G., *Folkways,* Ginn & Co., Boston, 1906.

Trow, W. C., ed., *Character Education in Soviet Russia,* Paul Kalachov, trans., Ann Arbor Press, Michigan, 1934.

U.S. Commissioner of Education, *Report of the Commissioner of Education,* Washington, Government Printing Office, June 30, 1918, and every June 30 onwards.

U.S. Office of Education, *Soviet Commitment to Education* (Report of the First Official U.S. Education Mission to the USSR), U.S. Government Printing Office, Washington, 1959.

Webb, Sidney and Beatrice, *Soviet Communism—A New Civilization?* 2 vols., Chas. Scribner's Sons, New York, 1936.

Whyte, W. F., *Street Corner Society: The Social Structure of an Italian Slum,* University of Chicago Press, Chicago, 1943.

Williams, F. E., *Russia, Youth and the Present Day World,* Farrar & Rinehart, New York, 1934.

Wilson, L., *The New Schools of New Russia,* Vanguard Studies of Soviet Russia (no printer or place), 1928.

Winn, R. B., ed. and trans., *Soviet Psychology: A Symposium,* Philosophical Library, New York, 1961.

Wolin, S., and Slusser, R. M., *The Soviet Secret Police,* Frederick Praeger, New York, 1957.

Woody, Thomas, *New Minds—New Men?* Macmillan, New York, 1932.

Zenkovsky, V. V., *A History of Russian Philosophy,* 2 vols., George Kline, trans., Columbia University Press, New York, 1953.

INDEX

Abortion, legalization of, 37
Alexander I, 20
Alexander II, 20

Besprizorniki: numbers of, 47; nature of the problem, 47–49; early provisions for, 48–49; connotation of the term, 50–57; characteristics of, 52–55; treatment of, 55–56; Makarenko's views on, 59–60; Makarenko's treatment of, 59–60. *See also* Orphans
Blonski, Pavel, 43, 58, 127, 139
Boards of Public Assistance (tsarist), 20
Bolsheviks: their educational legacy, 13; early educational efforts, 14–15; assumption of power in Russia, 25–26; early educational changes, 27–30
Book for Parents, A, 6, 11, 152, 157, 169, 171, 173–76, 182, 187, 190, 195
Brigade system: as an educational method, 144–45. *See also* Complex method, Project method
Bubnov, Andrei, 145

Catherine II, 20
"Challenge and response": as a technique of educational control, used by Makarenko, 102, 110, 166, 202, 208
Cheka. *See* Police, Soviet
Code of Laws Concerning the Civil Registration of Deaths, Births,

and Marriages (1918), 37, 184–85
Collective, the: the school as, 33; as an "ideal" social form, 82, 88; fundamental qualities of, 92, 112; achievement of in the colony, 114; endorsed by Krupskaya, 140; in conflict with individuality (Stakhanovism), 148–49; and absorption of the individual, 160, 162–63; the family considered as, 187
"Colony of the Cheerful Life," 138
Commission for the Establishment of Schools of 1782, 20
Competition: introduced by Makarenko into education, 85; criticism of Makarenko for his use of, 108; Makarenko's defense of, 128–29; as official Soviet policy (Stakhanovism), 148–49; as factor in bourgeois society, 176–77; in relation to discipline, 194. *See also* Stakhanovism
Complex method, 139–40, 141–43, 145
Conditioning, 103, 121, 168
Creativity and criticism: lack of in Makarenko's methods, 194, 204, 205, 207
Critical awareness, development of. *See* Creativity and criticism

Dalton plan: use of in Soviet education, 58, 140, 143, 144, 145

229